The Metabolism
Plan
Vegan & Vegetarian
COOKBOOK

ALSO BY LYN-GENET RECITAS

The Plan

The Plan Cookbook

The Metabolism Plan

The Metabolism
Plan
Vegan & Vegetarian
COOKBOOK

Over 150 low-inflammatory recipes
that will boost your metabolism

LYN-GENET RECITAS

New York Times
bestselling author of
The Plan and *The Metabolism Plan*

Lyn-Genet Press
New York

The advice herein is not intended to replace the services of trained health professionals or to be a substitute for medical advice. You are advised to consult with your healthcare professional with regard to matters relating to your health and, in particular, regarding matters that may require diagnosis or medical attention.

Copyright 2018 by Lyn-Genet Recitas

Lyn-Genet Press

Post Office Box 474

Dobbs Ferry, NY 10522

lyngenet.com

Printed and bound in the United States of America

First printing: October 2018

Second printing: December 2018

Names: Recitas, Lyn-Genet, author.
Title: The Metabolism Plan Vegan & Vegetarian Cookbook: More than 150 low-inflammatory
  recipes that will boost your metabolism / Lyn-Genet Recitas, *New York Times* bestselling
  author of *The Plan* and *The Metabolism Plan*.
Description: First Edition. | Lyn-Genet Press, 2018.
Identifiers: LCCN: 2018911271 | ISBN 9781732816503 (paperback) |
  ISBN 9781732816510 (ebook)
Subjects: BISAC: COOKING / Vegan | COOKING / Vegetarian | HEALTH & FITNESS / Diet
  & Nutrition / Weight Loss

This is a dedication of love

Thank you to my family, Brayden, Bill, Ella, and Ted. Also, a big shout out to my sisters in crime and laughter, Tracy, Sarah and Jaci. I love you all so much. To my awesome folks at The Plan- you guys rock and I love you- Laura, Saloni, Donna, Emily, Katie and Chauntele. Thanks for being my rock. I am inspired by you and the incredible people I am blessed to work with daily. To my Planners all over the world, I love you and your courage to make positive change every day in your life.

Contents

Introduction

This book is for YOU

A lot has changed since I wrote The Plan in 2013: gathering data from thousands more people from all over the world, creating *The Metabolism Plan*, and now *The Metabolism Plan Cookbook*. This cookbook was written for anyone who wants a plant-based diet and to consume the least inflammatory foods. The Metabolism Plan is the best method of finding healthy foods that cause inflammation, rapid weight gain and can hasten the aging process.

Wait, healthy foods make you fat? I know it's counterintuitive, but it's true. Healthy, low-calorie foods, like green beans, Greek yogurt, quinoa, black beans, cauliflower, and oatmeal, can result in a weight gain of one to two pounds. All the foods that I just listed are 85% reactive, which means that for 85% of the population over the age of 35, these foods will cause inflammation and weight gain.

This doesn't make sense. It's a calorie in and a calorie out, right? Wrong. Well, then, what *does* actually happen? The simplest answer is that any "healthy" food can trigger an inflammatory response. This inflammatory response triggers a domino effect that affects your digestion and, ultimately affects your immune system. That "healthy" spinach and egg white omelet may be prematurely aging you, expanding your waistline, and causing health issues.

What we all need to know is that we are all chemically unique; our weight and health are just our chemical reactions to food. We also need to remember that aging is a state of inflammation and that systems start to slow down as you get older. Your body simply can't repair as quickly as it did when you were younger. Digestive enzyme production slows down, and stomach acid and saliva levels decrease, which means that digestion slows down. Hormonal imbalances trigger yeast flare-ups that change our gut flora and hormones. The foods we used to be able to digest down easily in our teens and twenties are just more difficult to break down in our thirties, forties, fifties, and beyond.

When you eat healthy foods that don't work for YOUR chemistry, many systems are impacted. This inflammatory response can last up to 72 hours. Histamine is released, and cortisol levels rise, impacting long-term fat storage. Increased cortisol production negatively impacts hormones such as progesterone and testosterone.

The more cortisol you release, the more your hormonal balance is negatively affected. These hormonal fluctuations disrupt water balance, metabolism, thyroid health, and immune response. Elevated cortisol leads to increased blood sugar levels. Insulin spikes resulting from reactive foods increase yeast and alter your gut flora. Altered gut flora leads to a compromised immune response, and the balance of your intestinal bacteria is thrown off. Remember that the majority of your immune system is in your gut! It's a rapid interplay and domino effect that affects your stress levels, moods, health, and immune system. And oh, by the way, you're gaining weight.

The Effects of Reactive Foods on Your Body

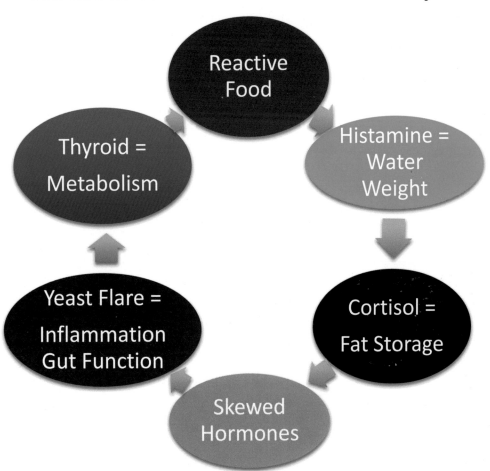

Figure 1: The Effects of Reactive Foods on Your Body

If you are trying to eat healthfully most of the time, and your health and weight are simply not responding, it might be time to find out why your efforts are not paying off as they should. So, if you haven't read *The Metabolism Plan*, please do!

Will this cookbook be good for you even if you haven't read *The Metabolism Plan*? The simple answer is yes. I have included all the least reactive foods based on my findings, and so pretty much every ingredient included in this book is 30% reactive or lower.

Another important factor for your best health and weight is exercise. *The Metabolism Plan* also helps you find the exercise that works for YOUR body. Over-training, or doing the wrong types of exercise for your body, can slow your metabolism and wreak havoc on your hormones.

There is one more reason to read this book. I remember being a shy, sickly child with numerous migraines each month. My one source of comfort were my books. The doctors I saw for my migraines and heart palpitations could not help me. So, at a very young age, I started to read books about health. These books were so thrilling to me! These books taught me that everything that grows on this planet has the potential to heal you. I believe that to this day, and this is the foundation of my life's work. Food not only nourishes you; but also all foods, herbs and spices contain potent compounds that reverse disease, make you happier, and, yes, be at your best weight. I hope this book inspires you to try new vegetables, spices and herbs and to remember that eating should be joyful.

Over-training Can Slow Weight Loss

I have been compiling information on how people respond to exercise for over 10 years and have found that although some of us have the genetics to be an athlete, most of us do not. Response to exercise over the age of 40 drastically changes from when we were younger:

- Women and men over the age of 40 who exercise 5-6 days a week generally lose 25% less weight than those who exercise 3-4 times a week.

- People who exercised every other day had the best weight-loss results.

- Exercising for more than 20–30 minutes (30–40 minutes for men) often slowed weight loss or caused weight gain.

- The biggest culprits are boot camp, CrossFit-style classes, Hot yoga, and spinning.

- Walking more than 8,000 steps per day may be perceived as stress by the body.

While people may be tempted to say that this weight gain could be attributed to muscle growth, I have found that the days where there is weight gain from exercise, there is also a corresponding exacerbation of people's health issues: thyroid function decreases, while insulin levels and blood pressure may rise.

Over-training has been shown to decrease blood levels of l-glutamine, dopamine, and 5-HTP, which affect mood, energy, and the body's ability to repair. Excessive exercise can negatively affect thyroid function and slow your metabolism. That's not why you exercise! Once you affect your thyroid, you are hitting a master gland that regulates everything - from your energy levels, mood, sex drive, hormonal responses, and ability to lose weight (just to name a few of the functions!). In addition, over-exercising will increase cortisol levels, which increases insulin output and encourages fat storage. In fact, cortisol can *suppress* your metabolism. The increase in cortisol depletes progesterone or testosterone levels, creating hormonal imbalances. Exercising for more than 30 minutes has been shown to increase leptin, your hunger hormone, thus offsetting the weight-loss benefits of exercise.

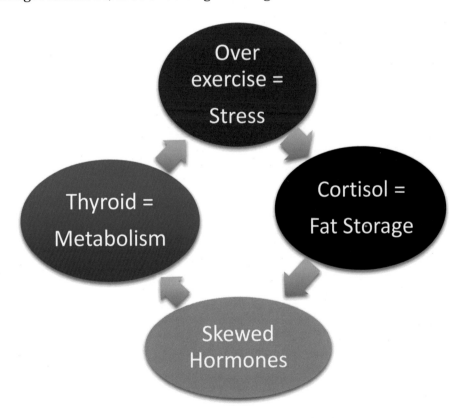

Figure 2: The Effects of Over-Exercise

In addition, as we age, the body's ability to withstand oxidative stress diminishes. Periods of constantly elevated heart rate seem to cause the most damage. Not allowing for adequate periods of rest after oxidative stress can heighten inflammation. Excess oxidative stress can cause cancer, heart disease, and type 2 diabetes.

You deserve to know which exercises support your body and *The Metabolism Plan* can teach you.!

Goitrogens and Your Metabolism

I mention goitrogens quite a bit in this book. Goitrogens are foods that have a negative effect on thyroid function if consumed too often. As your thyroid is a major player in your metabolism and every metabolic and cellular function, you want to keep it happy! So, the myth that metabolism slows as you age is just that. A myth. You have control over your metabolism, and it's so much easier than you think. You can start by rotating how often you eat these healthy foods.

What are goitrogens?

Goitrogens are compounds that disrupt thyroid function by interfering with one of the most vital nutrients for your metabolism, iodine. Your thyroid is an organ that is directly responsible for your metabolism, digestion, and mood. In addition, your thyroid is a major player when it comes to hormonal health, as it stimulates and synchronizes the metabolic and cellular functions in every tissue in your body. It is estimated that almost 60 million people in the US, and over 200 million people worldwide, have thyroid dysfunction and that many of these cases go undiagnosed.

Are you suffering from any of these symptoms?

- Weight gain
- Depression
- Anxiety
- Hair loss
- Low sex drive
- Feeling cold

- Hormonal imbalance
- Sleep issues
- Constipation, IBS
- Low energy
- Foggy thinking
- Carb and sugar cravings

If you have these symptoms, then there's a good sign that your thyroid may not be functioning optimally, even if your bloodwork comes back as "normal" (and I explain why thyroid tests are often inaccurate in *The Metabolism Plan*).

Here's the irony: Some of the healthiest foods are goitrogens. The very foods you are trying to program into your healthy diet can be the very reason your waistline is expanding and the reason you aren't feeling well.

Here's a partial list of common goitrogens:

- Strawberries
- Spinach
- Raw kale
- Cabbage
- Brussels sprouts
- Cauliflower
- Sweet potato
- Peaches
- Mustard
- Peanut butter
- Arugula
- Soy

Does this mean that you should avoid these foods completely? No, but you do want to make sure you rotate them. Most goitrogens are wonderful to consume once a week. This allows your body to reap all the health benefits while still being able to break down any problematic compounds. In fact, one of the main tenets of *The Metabolism Plan* is "rotate or react."

You see, if you eat a food too often, the various compounds in the food can start to overwhelm your body, causing food sensitivities as well as health and weight issues. Your reaction could range from simple bloating after a meal to weight gain, depression, constipation, joint pain, or headaches. Left unchecked, consuming goitrogens too often can cause health issues like type 2 diabetes and autoimmune diseases.

Soaking Your Seeds, Grains, and Nuts

Seeds, grains, and nuts are an important source of vegan protein. However, as always, every food can cause problems if consumed too often. Seeds and grains contain phytic acid, which impairs the absorption of important minerals, such as calcium, iron, and zinc. Luckily, soaking them overnight and then rinsing them can reduce levels of phytic acid. This process also makes the nutrients more bio-available, neutralizes enzyme inhibitors, and encourages the production of enzymes to ease digestion. Cooking reduces phytic acid levels even more.

Soaking beans is also recommended. I do discuss a quick method in the book, because, hey, sometimes, you just don't have the time to soak. If you do soak your beans, however, it will increase your ability to digest legumes because the gas-causing enzymes and trisaccharides in legumes are released. You are going to find that I talk about digestion a LOT because whenever you aid digestion and gut health, you support your immune system and production of serotonin (your "I'm happy" hormone)!

Water

Water is needed for every cellular function, and most people are chronically dehydrated, which substantially slows weight loss and repair. Your baseline is half your body weight in ounces; therefore, the best way to do this is to drink a pint all at once. Please drink water in between meals, not during, as drinking during meals can impair your digestion. A 45-minute window before and after each meal would be ideal. Try to finish all water an hour before dinner or 3-4 hours before bed. Please do not drink over the recommended water amount as this may affect kidney function and may cause water retention. That is a lousy way to gain weight!

Why Am I Gaining So Much Weight on A Gluten-Free Diet?

While many people may believe that they have gluten intolerance (with many finding out, through *The Metabolism Plan*, that they don't), gluten-free products can be just as problematic. The alternative grains used are often reactive and will continue to negatively affect digestion and weight. Here are some reasons why that can happen.

Two major ingredients in gluten-free bread are tapioca starch and potato starch. Tapioca starch is highly inflammatory, and potato starch has been linked to various disorders such as arthritis, eczema, psoriasis, and fibromyalgia. Thus, when foods trigger inflammatory diseases, an uptick on the scale is probable. In fact, it's the starch of the potato that cause the most weight gain.

Grains such as quinoa and teff are 70% reactive. If your ancestors have never been exposed to these grains, your body may not possess the enzymes to break them down. The body responds best to what has been part of your genetic past, teff is from Ethiopia and quinoa from the Andes. Naturally, therefore, if you are from either of these regions, you have a better chance of digesting these grains.

Corn is 90% reactive and is often genetically modified. Even if you buy organic corn, GMO may still be a problem. Experts fear that cross-pollination has already begun with GMO corn, as the pollen grains are among the largest and heaviest of wind-pollinated plants. I often see clients gain a pound from the simple pleasure of corn on the cob. Corn also contains a compound known as zein, which can create a very similar immune response as gluten.

Please avoid brown rice flour products for regular use, as the arsenic content is high. Consuming brown rice or brown rice flour would be best limited to several times a month.

So, what does this mean if you can't tolerate gluten? That you shouldn't have any sort of bread at all? That's not the purpose of this information. I'm really not here to torture you! What I DO want you to know is that if you find that your body is not responding the way it should, then gluten-free products might be the problem. Try to avoid daily ingestion of these products and give your body a chance to rest and decrease its inflammatory response. I have found coconut flour and almond flour to be the most easily digested; thus, the GF recipes here feature those ingredients.

It's also important to remember that just because something is pro-inflammatory for a certain population, it does NOT mean that it's going to be a problem for you. Just listen to your body - it will tell you everything you need to know!

The flours and breads I have listed here are the least reactive gluten containing products: spelt flour, 00 flour from Italy, sourdough bread, and pita. Sourdough bread is fermented, making it easier to digest. Some people with yeast or candida can react better to pita or lavash, as both are lower in yeast.

Chia and Flax

Chia and flax are great sources of vegan protein, and are also a wonderful source of omega 3 and calcium. Some people, however, find that these two seeds do best as a breakfast option. These two nutritional powerhouses have an expansive quality, which may slow digestion if you already have food on your stomach. So, note how you feel if you have them later in the day.

Protein

I do find that many of the vegans and vegetarians I am working with are not getting enough protein or are not sufficiently rotating their protein sources. I have devised this cookbook to make sure that your breakfasts, lunches, and dinners have enough protein for optimal health and weight. You will note, that with a recipe, I may suggest adding a pesto, grains, seeds, cheese, etc. The reason is because I want to make sure that YOU get enough protein to fuel your wonderful life.

How This Cookbook Can Help

There are two crucial steps to achieving the healthy body you have always wanted: Reset your system by doing The Cleanse (or all 30 days), and then find the foods that work for *your* body. Not your best friend's body. Not your trainer's body. Not some Instagram star's body. Not even your sister's body. Remember this motto: What's healthy for me may not be healthy for you.

Our planet is unique, in that everything we need for our optimal health is right here. The plants, seeds, and herbs that grow, nourish us in so many ways. Find the foods that work for your body to heal you. Food is truly your medicine.

Reset your system

Eating the foods that work well with your body enables it to reach homeostasis. Your body constantly wants to repair, but it will always divert energy from repair to digestion. If you eat a food that doesn't work for your chemistry, that inflammatory response can last up to 72 hours. You can quickly see how eating just three reactive foods a week can start to slow your body's energy to repair. This means declining health and weight gain. But you can stop this process and turn back the clock!

In this book, you will learn the steps to complete the Three-Day Cleanse, during which you will eat the foods I have found to be least reactive. If you've already done The Metabolism Plan, you know which foods work best for you. If you haven't tried it, I highly recommend going through the 30 days and find the healthy foods that work for you and the ones that don't. Not ready for that commitment just yet? All the recipes in this book contain the foods that I've found to be the least inflammatory and that work to boost your metabolism by supporting thyroid health.

I am going to include the Vegan Three-Day Cleanse based on *The Metabolism Plan* so that you get an idea of how powerful this can be. You see, your body always wants to heal and have you at your best weight. When you eat the foods that work for your body, it will do just that! The foods you eat over this three-day period will help you lose weight and reset your body back to healing. Average weight loss is 5–10 pounds in three days, even though you are eating over 2,000 calories a day if you are a woman and over 2,500 if you are a man!

This cookbook has over 150 recipes that contain the foods that I've found to be the least inflammatory overall. These are the foods that most people can tolerate well and that don't cause an inflammatory response.

For those of you who are new to Planning and who don't want to jump in with all 30 days, start with The Cleanse. Afterwards, try the recipes in this book, and note how you feel. Does your energy dip after a meal? Are you gassy, bloated, or do you have an energy dip? Try to avoid those reactive foods. Does a dish make you feel fantastic? Is your stomach flat and your mood and digestion great? Then those are going to be your foundational foods.

The Vegan Three-Day Cleanse

In the morning of each day of The Cleanse, please remember to:

#1 Weigh yourself after you urinate. I say this in all my books - the scale is your best friend. It is going to end the mystery of why you gain weight. That number on the scale? It's just data. It lets you know what to keep in and what to kick to the curb. When you reach your goal weight, you should just stabilize there! Your weight reflects information from the prior day's stimulus of food, water, stress, and exercise.

#2 Start your day off with a pint of water with lemon after you weigh yourself. That lemon water aids liver health. Your liver is responsible for over 500 functions, such as balancing hormones and maintaining a revved-up metabolism. If you can, don't have coffee during The Cleanse, and give your body a little break from caffeine.

Vegan Three Day Cleanse: *Women's Menu*

Note: All salads should include a dressing of EVOO and lemon juice.

Day One:

Breakfast

- 1 cup Flax Granola (page 31) with ½ cup blueberries
- Coconut milk or rice milk

Lunch

- 2 cups Carrot Ginger Soup (page 48) with a handful of sunflower seeds
- 2 cups sautéed or steamed broccoli with EVOO and drizzle of lemon juice
- Baby romaine or green leaf lettuce with ½ pear, EVOO and drizzle of lemon juice

Snack

- 1 apple

Dinner

- 10 cups sautéed kale, 3-4 carrots, 1 onion, 1 zucchini, 4 shiitakes, and 4 cups broccoli with ½ cup Spicy Coco Sauce (page 136). This is 2 portions.
- Grated carrot and raw grated beet salad with a handful of pumpkin seeds

Day Two:

Breakfast

- 1 cup Flax Granola (page 31) with ½ cup blueberries
- Coconut milk or rice milk

Lunch

- 2 cups Carrot Ginger Soup (page 48) with a handful of sunflower seeds
- 2 cups sautéed or steamed broccoli with EVOO and drizzle of lemon juice
- Baby romaine or green leaf lettuce with ½ diced apple, EVOO and drizzle of lemon juice

Snack

- 1 pear with 8 almonds

Dinner

- Leftover sautéed kale and veggies with 1 cup basmati rice and pumpkin seeds
- Beet/carrot salad with sunflower seeds

Vegan Three Day Cleanse: Women's Menu (cont.)

Day Three: Lentils

Breakfast

- 1 cup Flax Granola (page 31) with ½ cup blueberries or ½ pear
- Coconut milk or rice milk

Lunch

- Baby romaine or green leaf lettuce with carrots and pumpkin seeds with EVOO and drizzle of lemon juice
- 2 cups Cream of Broccoli Soup (page 51)

Snack

- 12–15 almonds

Dinner

- 1 cup cooked lentils with 2 cups cooked kale
- The Cleanse Oven-Roasted Vegetables (page 111) finished with EVOO, lemon juice and fresh black pepper
- Baby romaine with 1 handful of sunflower seeds, EVOO and a drizzle of lemon juice

Vegan Three Day Cleanse: *Men's Menu*

Note: All salads should include a dressing of EVOO and lemon juice.

Day One

Breakfast

- 1½ cups Flax Granola (page 31) with 1 cup blueberries
- Coconut milk or rice milk

Lunch

- 2½ cups Carrot Ginger Soup (page 48)
- 2½ cups sautéed or steamed broccoli, drizzled with EVOO and lemon juice
- Baby romaine or green leaf lettuce with 1½ oz. sunflower seeds, EVOO and a drizzle of lemon juice

Snack

- 1 apple

Dinner

- 12 cups sautéed kale, 3-4 carrots, 1 onion, 1 zucchini, 4 shiitakes, and 4 cups broccoli with 1 cup Spicy Coco Sauce (page 136). This is 2 portions.
- Grated carrot and raw grated beet salad with a handful of pumpkin seeds

Day Two: Almonds

Breakfast

- 1½ cups Flax Granola (page 31) with 1 cup blueberries
- Coconut milk or rice milk

Lunch

- 2½ cups Carrot Ginger Soup (page 48) with 1.5 oz. sunflower seeds
- Baby romaine or green leaf lettuce with ½ diced apple, ½ avocado, EVOO and a drizzle of lemon juice
- 2½ cups steamed or sautéed broccoli, drizzled with EVOO and lemon juice

Snack

- 1 pear with 16 almonds

Dinner

- Leftover sautéed kale and veggies with 1½ cups basmati rice and 1½ oz. pumpkin seeds
- Beet/carrot salad with 1½ oz. sunflower seeds, EVOO and a drizzle of lemon juice

Vegan Three Day Cleanse: Men's Menu (cont.)

Day Three: Lentils

Breakfast

- 1½ cups Flax Granola (page 31) with 1 cup blueberries or 1 pear
- Coconut milk or rice milk

Lunch

- Baby romaine with carrots, 1½ oz. sunflower seeds, EVOO and a drizzle of lemon juice
- 2½ cups Cream of Broccoli Soup (page 51)

Snack

- 18–20 almonds

Dinner

- 1½ cups cooked lentils with 3 cups cooked kale
- The Cleanse Oven-Roasted Vegetables (page 111) finished with EVOO, lemon juice, and fresh black pepper
- Baby romaine or green leaf lettuce with EVOO and a drizzle of lemon juice

Inflammatory Foods

The immune system's response to an inflammatory diet is a diversion of the body's energy from healing and repair. It allows whatever is latent in our genetic makeup to "kick up" or worsen whatever is chronic (arthritis, migraines, depression, etc.).

Chronic inflammation exacerbates and hastens the aging process because it floods tissues with free radicals and promotes the destruction of normal cells. Research shows that this is a major contributor to the aging of the cardiovascular and nervous system. Inflammation is now recognized as one of the key risk factors for heart disease, diabetes, high cholesterol, stroke, and cognitive and neurological disorders.

The following table is the list, based on my own research, of many vegetarian foods that are consumed daily and their potential for reactivity:

Vegetarian Food Reactivity Table

85+% reactive	**60–70% reactive**	**50% reactive**	**5% or less reactive**
•Corn •Hard boiled eggs •Roasted nut butters •Bananas (women) •Sweet potatoes (women) •Wheat gluten (fake meat) •Yeast extract •Sushi rice **85% reactive** •Eggplant •Oatmeal •Greek yogurt •Black beans •Cannellini beans •Cauliflower •Cabbage •Asparagus •Powdered stevia •Coconut oil •Kombucha (store bought) •Bagels •Strawberries •Tomato sauce (with citric acid) •Cow's milk (pasteurized) •Whey •Dairy cheese •Green juices drunk daily	•Yogurt, regular •Green beans •Quinoa, teff •Gluten-free flour •Savoy cabbage •Bok choy •Celery •Portobello, button mushrooms •Cow's Cheese (except for Parmesan) •Pineapple •Grapefruit •Artichokes •Oranges •Almond milk (store bought) •Spaghetti squash, kabocha •Gluten-free bread •Soy •Pine nuts •Sesame seeds •Tahini •Cucumber •Celery •Romaine hearts, iceberg lettuce •Peppers •Tomatoes •Broccoli rabe, broccolini •Mustard •Sweet potato (men) •Melon (except watermelon) •Protein powders •Kiwi	•Couscous, farro •All other beans, including edamame •Rice flour •Peas •Dates **30–40% reactive** •Eggs •Lentils •Pintos •Chickpeas •Brussels sprouts •Pumpkin •Mung beans **20% reactive** •Snow peas •Sourdough, pita or lavash bread •Tempeh •Peanuts •Brown/green lentils •Millet, buckwheat •Blackberries •Cashews •Watermelon •Low-reactive tomato sauce •Butternut squash **10–15% reactive** •Potatoes •Delicata squash •Raspberries •Pomegranate •Pecans •Hemp seeds	•Pitted fruits (mango, avocado, etc.) •Garlic, onions, chives, leeks, etc. •Shiitaki and Asian mushrooms •Radicchio, endive, frisée •Red leaf, green leaf, Bibb lettuces •Fennel •Goat cheese •Sheep cheese •Broccoli •Carrots •Kale •Zucchini, yellow squash •Raw beets •Raw sunflower •Raw pumpkin seeds •Raw almonds •Apples •Pears •Blueberries •Chia seeds •Flax seeds •Coconut milk, rice milk •Organic spinach •Swiss chard •Wild rice, brown and basmati rice •Arugula •Cranberries

Figure 3: Vegetarian Food Reactivity Table

Abbreviations used in this book

(DF)   dairy-free recipe

EVOO extra-virgin olive oil

(GF)   gluten-free recipe

tbsp   tablespoon

tsp   teaspoon

(V)   vegan recipe

TMP   *The Metabolism Plan*

Breakfast

Almond Flour Apple Streusel (GF)

For those of you who are new to almond flour, blanched almond flour will produce a much lighter texture. You can make your own almond flour in a food processor with blanched almonds. To make this vegan, you can substitute avocado oil for butter. Almonds are often considered one of the best foods for brain function, thanks to L-carnitine and B2, which support neurological activity and prevent cognitive decline.

Streusel Topping

- 1½ cups blanched almond flour
- 1 tbsp brown sugar
- ¼ cup (½ stick) unsalted butter (softened)
- 1 tsp ground cinnamon
- 4 tbsp almond slivers

Apple Filling

- 3 apples, cored and chopped into ½-inch pieces
- 1 tsp ground cinnamon
- 1 tsp lemon juice
- ½ tsp cardamom
- ¼ tsp ground cloves

Special equipment: 4 x 8-oz. Mason jars

1. Preheat oven to 350 °F. Lightly butter the 4 Mason jars.
2. For the streusel: use a medium bowl and mix all the ingredients by hand or with a hand mixer. Set aside.
3. For the filling: combine all ingredients in a medium bowl and mix well.
4. Divide apple mixture evenly among the 4 buttered Mason jars. Top with ½ inch streusel topping, packing down firmly. Place Mason jars on a baking sheet to prevent toppling over.
5. Bake for 25 to 30 minutes until streusel topping is lightly browned.
6. Serve warm. Top with almond slivers.

Almond Apple Streusel

Apple Chia Compote with Flax Granola (V) (GF)

Restarting your Day 1–30 of the Metabolism Plan and The Cleanse? Want a change from flax for your breakfast, but LOVE how it aids digestion and keeps you full? Why not make a cinnamon apple chia compote and top it with 3-4 tbsp of flax granola?

Apples are rich in antioxidants like quercetin and phytonutrients that can help fight cancer, diabetes, and heart disease. Apples are also rich in pectin, which aids digestive health and can lower cholesterol.

What about the peel? Most of the fiber and antioxidants are in the skins, so please save time peeling, and instead eat the nutrients that are on the skins of apples and other vegetables and fruits. Why buy vitamin supplements when you can get everything you need from food?

- 2 cups chopped apples
- 2 cups coconut milk or rice milk
- 1 cup chia seeds
- 1 tbsp agave or honey
- 1 tsp pure vanilla extract
- ½ tsp cinnamon
- ½ tsp cardamom

Toppings

- flax granola (page 31)
- chopped apple (⅓ cup per serving)

1. Combine all the ingredients (except toppings) in a small saucepan and bring to a boil.

2. Reduce heat and let simmer for 2-3 minutes, stirring constantly to prevent the chia from coagulating.

3. Let sit for 5 minutes for soft compote and 10 minutes for firmer compote.

4. Top with flax granola and chopped apple.

5. Serve warm.

Apple Pie Bread (GF)

Your house will smell like Thanksgiving when you bake this! This recipe does not contain baking powder (and many of my baking recipes do not), because some people note that it can cause bloating. Cardamom is one of my favorite spices. It's so fragrant, is a natural diuretic, and is rich in antioxidants.

- 2 cups blanched almond flour
- 1 tbsp coconut flour
- 1 tsp ground cinnamon
- 1 tsp cardamom
- ½ tsp baking soda
- ¼ tsp cloves
- ¼ tsp sea salt
- ⅓ cup full fat coconut milk
- 4 tbsp avocado oil
- 6 tbsp honey

- 2 eggs
- ½ tsp vanilla extract
- 1 cup diced apples
- ⅓ cup pecans (chopped)

Crumb Topping:

- ¼ cup almond flour
- 1 tsp avocado oil
- ½ tsp cinnamon
- 1 tbsp pecans (chopped)

1. Preheat oven to 350 °F. Grease the bottom and sides of a 6.4 x 3.8-inch loaf pan with avocado oil, and line it with a piece of parchment paper. Cut paper to fit lengthwise, leaving some excess on the edges. You can also use an 8½ x 4½-inch medium loaf pan.

2. Mix the almond flour, coconut flour, cinnamon, cardamom, baking soda, cloves and sea salt.

3. In a separate bowl, whisk together the coconut milk, avocado oil, honey, eggs, and vanilla extract.

4. Mix the dry and wet ingredients just until combined. Do not over mix.

5. Gently fold the diced apple and chopped pecans into the batter.

6. Pour the batter into the prepared loaf pan.

7. In a bowl, mix all the crumb topping ingredients then sprinkle on batter. Bake for approximately 45-50 minutes.

8. Let bread cool. Remove the bread from the pan, slice, and serve warm.

Blueberry Compote (V)

This is a *Plan* staple, you can use this during The Cleanse to replace flax granola. This freezes REALLY well, so feel free to make big batches. All berries besides blueberries are a test, blackberries and raspberries are low in reactivity, while strawberries are highly reactive. Blueberries are rich in antioxidants and help to reduce DNA damage, which can slow the aging process and can protect against cancer.

- 4 cups blueberries
- 1 to 1¼ cups water
- ½ cup chia seeds
- 1 tbsp agave

- Cinnamon to taste, suggested ½ tsp; you can add cardamom, nutmeg, and cloves (all great digestive aids)

1. Simmer all the ingredients in a pot with water for 8-10 minutes. Stir frequently to prevent the chia from coagulating.
2. Serve warm or refrigerate.

Oregano and Cheese Bread

Oregano is one of my favorite herbs. First, it grows like a weed, so I look like some magical gardener. Second, it has such incredible health benefits, from boosting your immune system to being antifungal and anti-inflammatory. It's also a yeast fighter.

This recipe is for a bread maker (I am so in love with mine), but you could easily alter this recipe so that you won't have to use one.

- 3 cups bread flour
- 1 cup water
- ½ cup freshly grated cheese (Romano or Parmesan)
- 3 tbsp sugar

- 1 tbsp dried-leaf oregano
- 1½ tbsp EVOO
- 1 tsp salt
- 2 tsp active dry yeast

1. Prepare the bread in the bread machine using the dough cycle.
2. Once finished, bake in a preheated 375 °F oven for 25-30 minutes or until golden brown.

Brunch Frittata "Muffins" (GF)

How much do I love this recipe? These egg muffins freeze very well, as do most of my breakfasts, saving you precious time.

Eggs are great for vegetarians as they are an excellent source of vitamin B12. This is so important for energy levels and thyroid health. B12 helps to produce red blood cells and offset anemia. It's also a vital nutrient to improve mood and fight depression.

Originally cow's milk was only from A2 cows, but most of what is commercially available in the United States is from A1 cows. The A2 protein is closer to the proteins in breast milk, goat and sheep milk, making it easier to digest for many.

- 8 large eggs
- ¼ cup whole milk (A2) or coconut milk
- ¼ cup broccoli florets
- 2 tsp finely chopped chives
- ½ tsp celery seed
- ½ tsp chipotle
- ½ tsp salt
- ½ tsp freshly ground black pepper
- ¾ cup grated Manchego
- ¼ cup chopped red onions
- Small basil leaves for garnish (optional)

1. Preheat the oven to 350 °F. Line a standard-sized, 12-well muffin pan with baking paper cups or oil the muffin pan.

2. Whisk the eggs and milk until well blended, then mix in the broccoli, chives, and spices. Place approximately 2 tbsp of Manchego at the bottom of each muffin cup, and one teaspoon of the red onion, then evenly distribute the egg mixture among them so that each cup is about three-quarters full.

3. Bake (middle rack) for about 30 minutes, until the frittatas are set.

4. Serve immediately, garnished with basil, if desired. Alternatively, allow them to cool to room temperature before storing or freezing.

Buckwheat Pancakes (V) (GF)

Buckwheat flour is often included in lists of grains, but buckwheat is a seed from a plant. Studies show that even in high doses, buckwheat flour causes no issue for people with celiac disease.

Not only is it gluten-free, but it's an incredible vegan protein powerhouse, at 24 g of protein per cup. Protein is an important component of every cell in the body and is essential for repair and healing. Your body uses protein to make enzymes and hormones.

Buckwheat is rich in manganese, copper, iron, and magnesium. It's also a great source of phosphorus which plays an essential role in growth of tissues. The minerals in buckwheat are very bioavailable as it is low in phytic acid. This means your body can absorb its nutrients more easily.

- 2 chia 'eggs'[1] (2 tbsp chia seeds mixed with 6 tbsp warm water)
- 2 cups buckwheat flour
- 1 tsp baking powder
- ½ tsp cinnamon
- ¼ tsp cardamom
- A dash of sea salt
- ¼ cup apple sauce
- 2 cups coconut milk or rice milk
- Avocado oil (for pan)
- Optional: chopped pecans and berries

1. Make chia 'eggs' and set aside.
2. Combine the dry ingredients in a large bowl.
3. Combine the apple sauce and milk and stir in the chia eggs.
4. Add the wet ingredients to the dry ingredients and mix thoroughly.
5. Pour the batter onto an oiled skillet and cook over medium heat until browned on one side.
6. Flip pancakes and cook until browned on other side.
7. Serve warm with topping of choice.

---

[1] 1 chia egg = 1 tbsp chia seeds mixed with 3 tbsp warm water

Carrot Chia Muffins (GF)

If you are like me and prefer a breakfast that is lower in sugar and chock full of protein, this is the muffin for you! Cloves are antimicrobial and antibacterial, and studies have shown that they can kill E. coli.

Almonds are rich in vitamin E. Vitamin E is a powerful antioxidant that defends your cells against damage and prevents the artery-clogging oxidation of cholesterol. It also helps support the immune system and skin health. It also protects against toxins that can damage the eyes and brain and may help reduce damage from strokes and slow the effects of Alzheimer's.

Raisins are a good source of iron and aid digestion thanks to their fiber content. If you enjoy moderate to high intensity exercise than raisins are the dried fruit for you and are a great alternative for sports gels and chews (as long as you are properly hydrated). They are a quick source of carbohydrates and can help improve your athletic performance.

- 2¾ cups blanched almond flour
- ½ tsp baking soda
- 3 eggs
- ¼ cup chia seeds
- 6 tbsp butter
- ⅛ cup raisins
- 1 tsp vanilla
- 1¼ cups finely grated or shredded carrot
- 1 tbsp cinnamon
- ½ tsp ground ginger
- ¼ tsp ground cloves

1. Preheat oven to 350 °F.

2. Combine all the ingredients in a food processor and blend until thoroughly mixed, or for approximately 2 minutes.

3. Pour the mixture into the paper-lined muffin cups and bake for approximately 22–25 minutes.

Chia Fruit Jam (V) (GF)

Got fruit ready to go bad? This is the perfect rescue and a great way to take advantage of summer and fall bounty. This also makes great dessert toppings.

Chia is incredibly rich in fiber. One ounce contains 10 grams, and the mucilage it releases greatly aids digestion. Foods that are high in fiber help people to feel full for longer, and a high fiber diet has been shown to help with weight loss. Increased fiber intake has been shown to lower blood pressure and cholesterol levels. Fiber also helps to regulate the immune system and lower inflammation.

- 1 cup fruit
- 2 tbsp chia seeds
- 2 tbsp lemon juice or water
- 1 tbsp agave

1. Add the fruit and chia to a bowl with lemon juice or water and agave. Let it sit for 30 minutes. You may add more fruit for more thickness. Serve on bread or as a dessert topping. It's great with ice cream!

Cheddar Chive Muffin (GF)

Here is another option for your savory breakfasts, folks! It is gluten-free, low in sugar, and rich in protein. Goat cheese is much easier to digest than cow's cheese, as the molecules are smaller than cow's milk. Goat cheese is a better environmental option as well. Goats are smaller, take up less space, and eat less food. The foods they do eat are much more varied (weeds, herbs, shrubs, etc.), which is probably why goat milk is higher in nutrients.

- 4 cups blanched almond flour
- ½ tsp baking soda
- 4 large eggs
- 3 tbsp chopped chives or scallions
- 2 cups grated goat cheddar cheese, Manchego, or goat gouda

1. Using a food processor, combine the almond flour and baking soda.
2. Pulse in eggs until well combined.
3. Briefly pulse in chives and cheddar cheese.
4. Scoop a heaping ¼ cup of batter into each paper-lined muffin cup.
5. Bake at 350 °F for 25–30 minutes.
6. Serve warm, or let cool and freeze.

Chocolate Breakfast Cupcakes (GF)

Using almond flour is a wonderful way to get your recommended protein intake and help balance your blood sugar. Almonds are naturally rich in probiotics, which support digestion, mood, and immune function.

Chia is used as a binding agent and is rich in protein, calcium, magnesium, and fiber.

The zucchini not only adds potassium and fiber, but also makes these treats super moist. You might not want to let people know how healthy they are.

- 2½ cups almond flour
- ½ cup cocoa powder
- ½ tsp baking soda
- 3 eggs
- ¼ cup chia seeds

- 4 tbsp avocado oil or butter
- ½ cup agave or honey
- 1 tsp vanilla
- 1¼ cups grated zucchini

1. Preheat the oven to 350 °F.
2. Combine all ingredients in a food processor, thoroughly mixing them (roughly 2 minutes).
3. Butter the cupcake tins and pour in the batter.
4. Bake for 20–25 minutes.
5. Check the cupcakes with a toothpick. When cooked, the toothpick will come out clean.
6. Serve warm, or let cool and freeze.

Coconut Flour Pancakes (GF)

So many GF recipes call for gluten-free flour blends which is much more reactive (see page 8). Almond flour is low-reactive but there are still plenty of folks who have an almond sensitivity. Here is a great low-reactive recipe with coconut flour.

One question I am often asked is whether coconut flour and almond flour are interchangeable in recipes. Alas, they are not! Coconut flour requires a much higher egg-to-flour ratio to rise (often, 1 egg per 1 tbsp). Almond flour uses much less.

What is interesting about coconut is that every form of coconut tests differently. Thus, while coconut milk, coconut sugar, and coconut flour are less reactive forms, coconut flakes, coconut water, and coconut oil are more reactive. FYI: coconut water is from green young coconuts, while coconut milk is from the mature version.

- 4 tbsp coconut flour
- ¼ tsp baking powder
- ¼ tsp baking soda
- ¼ tsp sea salt
- ¼ tsp cinnamon
- ⅛ tsp cardamom
- 1 tbsp honey
- 4 eggs
- ½ cup coconut milk or rice milk
- Avocado oil for frying

1. Using a medium bowl, combine the coconut flour, baking powder, baking soda, sea salt, cinnamon, cardamom, and honey. Add in the eggs and milk and stir until completely combined and thick. This may take several minutes; the batter will thicken as you stir (you can also mix this in a blender or food processor).

2. Spoon the batter into an oiled skillet and smooth with a spoon. Cook over medium heat until lightly browned, flipping carefully. Transfer pancakes to a plate and add toppings of your choice.

Flax Granola (V) (GF)

A Plan staple, flax granola is chock full of protein, omega 3, calcium, and fiber. It is amazing for relieving constipation and incredibly inexpensive. You can make big batches as it stores well (approximately 4 weeks) if kept in a cool, dry place. Using the overnight method aids nutrient absorption.

- 1 cup water
- 2 cups whole flaxseeds
- 1 tbsp agave

- 2 tsp ground cinnamon
- 1 tsp pure vanilla extract
- ½ tsp nutmeg

1. Combine the water and flaxseeds in a medium-sized bowl and mix well. Let the mixture sit for at least 30 minutes (or overnight) and mix again.

2. Preheat the oven to 275 °F. Add the agave, cinnamon, vanilla, and nutmeg to the flaxseeds and mix thoroughly.

3. Spread the granola in a thin layer on a baking sheet and bake for 50 minutes. Reduce oven temperature to 225 °F. Cut granola sheet into clusters, flip, and bake an additional 30-40 minutes until thoroughly dry.

Gluten-Free Curry Crackers (V) (GF)

Have wheat issues? Want a protein-rich snack? Try this cracker recipe. Typical GF-crackers are so expensive, but these are budget-friendly. You can make a double or triple batch and freeze the extra dough.

- ⅓ cup almond flour
- 1 tbsp coconut flour
- ¼ cup pumpkin seeds
- 2 tbsp sunflower seeds
- 3 tbsp flaxseeds

- ½ tsp sea salt
- 1 tsp curry powder (page 126)
- 2 tbsp EVOO
- ¼ cup water

1. Pulse the almond flour and coconut flour in a food processor until well combined. Pulse in seeds, salt and curry powder (leave as a coarse grind for texture). Pulse in EVOO, then water.

2. Refrigerate the dough for 30 minutes allowing the dough to thicken. Roll it out between 2 pieces of parchment paper until ¼ inch (or less) thick. Cut it into 2-inch squares. If you don't have parchment paper, just use more almond flour for rolling.

3. Bake at 300 °F for 20-25 minutes. Serve or store.

Huevos Rancheros (GF)

This is a perfect dish for a festive brunch and a great option if you are on a corn-free diet. I usually serve this with the spicy cucumber Margarita (page 200).

Eggs are a rich source of folate which is involved in energy production in the brain. Research shows that low folate consumption is associated with cognitive dysfunction. In a study of nearly 1,000 seniors, those who had the highest folate consumption had the lowest rates of Alzheimer's disease.

Studies have also show that low folate levels are also linked to depression. Folate supports serotonin regulation. Serotonin is a neurotransmitter that helps the brain manage a variety of functions. Some research shows that taking folate and b-12 supplements can boost the efficacy of antidepressants. The good news? Eggs are a great source of b-12 too.

- 8 large eggs
- ⅛ cup water
- 2 tbsp EVOO
- 16 veggie chia crackers (page 41)

- ½ cup ranchero sauce (page 135)
- Optional: guacamole and a cheese of your choice

1. Whisk the eggs with the water in a mixing bowl. Heat a skillet over medium heat and add oil. Pour the eggs into the skillet and scramble to desired consistency.

2. Place 4 chia crackers per person and top with scrambled eggs and ranchero sauce.

3. Serve with additional optional toppings, if desired.

Huevos Rancheros, page 32

Lemon Blueberry Chia Muffins (GF)

This recipe is nut-free, so it's a perfect option for our Planners who want to avoid almonds! These bad boys pack approximately 8 g of protein per muffin. This is a popular muffin recipe and works well as a breakfast on the run.

I love the glass bottled organic lemon juice from Lakewood Organic. It is very reasonably priced, and you don't have to worry about waste or the plastic compounds leaching into your juice.

- ½ cup coconut flour
- ½ tsp baking soda
- Dash of sea salt
- 6 large eggs
- ½ cup chia
- ½ cup agave or honey

- ½ cup butter (softened)
- Juice of one lemon appx. 2 tsp
- Zest of ½ lemon
- 1 tbsp pure vanilla extract
- 1 cup blueberries (fresh or frozen)

1. Preheat oven to 350 °F.

2. Using a small bowl, combine the coconut flour, baking soda, and salt.

3. Using a separate large bowl, whisk the eggs, chia, agave, butter, lemon, lemon zest, and vanilla.

4. Mix the dry ingredients into the wet. Gently fold in the blueberries. Spoon the batter into a well-buttered muffin tin.

5. Bake for 20–25 minutes. Remove from oven. Let cool and serve.

Lemon Blueberry Chia Muffins, page 34

Lemon Buckwheat Waffles (V) (GF)

Waffles are a joy; but for those of us who are egg sensitive (yes, I am one!), recipes like this are a godsend. This is packed with protein, thanks to the buckwheat and chia. This recipe is baking powder free.

I remember being a little girl and reading about how Native American runners would run mile after mile with only chia as their energy source. You can only imagine how this sick little girl thought of these seeds as magical! Well, in fact, they are pretty darn cool.

Chia seeds are a nutritional powerhouse being rich in protein, omega 3, and fiber. The calcium content is pretty high at almost 20% of your RDA per ounce. The mucilage it releases when soaked really aids digestion. To note, people with serious digestive disorders like Crohn's and diverticulitis should only use seeds like chia under the daily, one-on-one care of a nutritionist until digestion is healed.

- 2 chia 'eggs' (2 tbsp chia seeds mixed with 6 tbsp warm water)
- 2 cups buckwheat flour
- ⅓ cup coconut flour
- 1 tsp baking soda
- 1 tsp vanilla
- 2 tbsp maple syrup
- ¼ cup apple sauce
- 1½ cups coconut milk or rice milk
- Zest and juice of 1 lemon

1. Begin heating the waffle iron.
2. Make chia 'eggs' and set aside.
3. Using a large bowl, combine the dry ingredients.
4. Combine the all of the ingredients in a bowl. Let batter sit for a few minutes to thicken, stirring occasionally.
5. When the waffle iron is hot, add ½ cup of batter and follow the waffle iron's cooking instructions.
6. Repeat until batter is used up.
7. Serve with toppings of choice, such as chopped apple and almonds.

Overnight Breakfast Bulgur Bowl (V) (GF)

This is a great recipe for folks, like me, who miss their oatmeal. Bulgur has high levels of iron, magnesium, potassium, zinc, niacin, copper, phosphorous, manganese, fiber, and protein.

In this book I mention coconut milk and rice milk as preferred non-dairy milks because they tend to be incredibly low reactive. Soy, hemp, and almond milk are much higher inflammatory.

Overnight bulgur "oats"

- 1 cup uncooked bulgur
- 1½ cups coconut milk or rice milk
- ¼ cup dried cranberries

Bulgur Breakfast

- ¼ cup nuts or seeds of choice
- ½ cup milk of choice
- 1 tsp ground cinnamon
- ½ tsp cardamom
- 1 chopped apple
- 2 tsp agave or honey

Overnight bulgur "oats"

1. Combine all the ingredients for the overnight "oats". Cover and refrigerate overnight.

Bulgur Breakfast

2. In the morning, combine the remaining ingredients with the overnight oats. Stir well.

3. Heat the mixture in a saucepan, or serve at room temp.

Pumpkin Pie Overnight Buckwheat Groats (V) (GF)

Here's another low-reactive alternative to oatmeal, that is gluten-free, hearty, and filling.

Buckwheat groats are rich in antioxidants. They lower cholesterol and aid digestion. They are also a great source of B vitamins and magnesium. One of magnesium's roles is to help muscles relax (think Epsom salts) which aids digestion. It also helps to decrease stress and anxiety and aids a nice, deep, restful sleep.

- ¼ cup raw buckwheat groats[2]
- 2 tbsp chia seeds
- ¼ tsp ground cinnamon
- 2 tsp agave or honey
- 1 tsp cinnamon
- ½ tsp cardamom
- ½ tsp nutmeg
- ½ tsp vanilla extract
- ½ cup milk of choice, more for simmering

Toppings:

- Dried cranberries, nuts, seeds (optional)

1. Rinse the groats under running water. Mix all the ingredients (except toppings) in a bowl until combined. Let the mixture sit overnight in the refrigerator.

2. Remove from refrigerator the next day. Stir well and then add groats to a sauce pan. Add extra milk and stir frequently until warm.

3. Add toppings and stir again for 1-2 minutes.

4. Heat in a pan and enjoy warm or at room temperature.

---

[2] Bob's Red Mill is a great option; usually found in the organic or gluten-free aisle (not Kasha).

Pumpkin Bread (GF)

This is great as a breakfast or snack. Pumpkin seeds are a rich source of zinc, which supports immune function and hormones. They also aid digestion and heart and liver health. For you workout fanatics, it also aids hypertrophy (muscle growth).

- 1 cup blanched almond flour
- ¼ tsp sea salt
- ½ tsp baking soda
- 1½ tsp cinnamon
- ½ tsp cardamom
- ½ tsp ginger
- ½ cup pumpkin seeds
- 3 tbsp agave or honey
- 3 large eggs
- ¼ cup pumpkin puree

1. Using a food processor, combine the almond flour, salt, baking soda, and spices.
2. Add the pumpkin seeds, honey, eggs, and pumpkin puree.
3. Pulse for 2 minutes. Scoop the batter into a mini loaf pan.
4. Bake at 350 °F for 35–45 minutes. Serve warm.

Pumpkin Pie Smoothie (V)

All the spices used for this recipe aid digestion. If you bloat easily, omit the ice from smoothies and consume at room temperature. Pumpkin is rich in fiber for optimal digestion and vitamin A for eye health and immune function.

- 1 cup coconut milk or rice milk
- 1 ripe pear or 1 cup applesauce
- ½ cup pumpkin puree
- 2 tbsp almond butter
- 2 tbsp chia seeds

- ½ tsp cinnamon
- ½ tsp ginger
- ½ tsp nutmeg
- ¼ tsp cloves

1. Combine all ingredients in a food processor or blender and blend until smooth.
2. Enjoy immediately.

Rice Pudding (V)

This warming breakfast is great for fueling your morning workout. Serve with nuts or seeds of your choice to boost protein.

Basmati rice is lower in arsenic than other rice varieties. Arsenic is a heavy metal that inhibits your body's ability to utilize minerals that are essential for optimal thyroid health.

You can find rose water in Middle Eastern stores.

- 2 cups cooked basmati rice
- 1 cup coconut milk or rice milk
- ¼ cup raisins
- 1 tsp cinnamon
- ½ tsp cardamom

- ½ tsp nutmeg
- ½ tsp rose water or vanilla extract
- ½ cup crushed pecans or almond slivers

1. Combine all the ingredients in a medium-sized saucepan and simmer over low heat, stirring frequently for 3-4 minutes, until well mixed and fragrant. Top with pecans and enjoy immediately.

Veggie (Chia) Crackers (V) (GF)

This recipe is awesome for simple, inexpensive, gluten-free crackers that have the perfect crunch! It's also a great way to sneak in extra veggies. On top of that, the high fiber content will keep you full and help lower cholesterol.

Beets can lower blood pressure, improve digestion, and fight cancer. They can boost athletic performance by improving oxygen use and endurance. Athletes find that consuming beet juice or beets 2-3 hours before competing had the best effects.

Part of beet's color comes from a pigment called betalain, which has shown to be anti-inflammatory. One study showed that betalain capsules made from beets reduced pain and inflammation associated with arthritis.

Carrot Crackers

- 2 cups grated carrot
- 2 tbsp flaxseed
- 3 tbsp chia seeds
- ½ tsp onion powder
- Dash sea salt

Beet Crackers

- 2 cups grated beet
- 2 tbsp flaxseed
- 3 tbsp chia seeds
- ½ tsp garlic powder
- Dash sea salt

Baking

- ¼ cup EVOO for oiling 2 baking sheets

1. Place all the Carrot Cracker ingredients into a food processor and blend. Scrape down the sides to incorporate all the ingredients. Form the mixture into a ball and let sit for 45 minutes for mucilage to form, which binds the ingredients. Repeat the process for the Beet Cracker ingredients.

2. Preheat the oven to 225 °F and oil the baking sheets.

3. Take 2 sheets of parchment paper and place the carrot dough between them. Use a rolling pin to roll out the dough until it is ⅛-inch thick. Use a 4-inch round cookie cutter to form the crackers. Repeat the process for the beet dough. Place the crackers onto cookie sheets and bake for 50 minutes. Flip the crackers and bake for an additional 50 minutes. For extra crispy crackers, turn off the oven and leave the crackers in for 1 hour.

Warm Cranberry Flax Cereal (V) (GF)

Flax granola is a Plan favorite. It's amazing for digestion, thanks to its mucilage, and is also a great source of protein, calcium, and omega 3. However, making the Flax granola is a bit time consuming, so this quick recipe is perfect for the time crunched. It's a hearty and warming breakfast. Please limit flax consumption to twice weekly. as it's a phytoestrogen.

- 1 cup flaxseed
- 1 cup water
- ½ cup coconut milk or rice milk
- ¼ cup dried cranberries
- 1 tbsp honey
- 1 tsp cinnamon
- ½ tsp cardamom
- ½ tsp ginger

1. Soak the flax overnight in a bowl of water.

2. The next day, add 1 cup of soaked flax, coconut milk or rice milk, cranberries, honey, cinnamon, cardamom and ginger to a saucepan.

3. Simmer for 1-2 minutes. Serve warm.

Warm Spelt Flakes with Mango (V) (GF)

Bob's Red Mill makes great spelt flakes. You can also purchase spelt flakes in bulk from health food stores for even greater savings. Spelt can be much easier to digest than traditional US or Canadian wheat.

- 4 cups spelt flakes
- 3 cups water
- 1 cup chopped mango (fresh or frozen)
- ½ cup blueberries (fresh or frozen)
- 1 tbsp agave or honey
- 1 tsp fresh lemon juice
- 1 tsp cinnamon
- ½ tsp ginger
- ¼ cup rice or coconut milk

1. Using a large bowl, soak the spelt flakes in water overnight in the refrigerator. Soaking makes the spelt flakes even more digestible. Remove the spelt flakes from the refrigerator in the morning and heat in a small saucepan for 3-4 minutes.

2. Combine the mango, blueberries, honey, lemon juice, cinnamon, ginger, and milk in a small saucepan.

3. Bring the mixture to a boil over high heat. Lower the heat and simmer until the fruit is soft and the liquid thickened (about 15 minutes).

4. Serve over warm spelt cereal.

Salads and Soups

Apple Salad with Raspberry Vinaigrette and Mint (V)

What could be an easier or more refreshing salad?

Researchers have found that Granny Smith apples, compared to all other apples, have the biggest impact on good gut bacteria, which means a better immune system, better gut function, and happier mood.

Lemon balm is a wonderful herb in the mint family which helps to lower high blood pressure and reduce anxiety.

Raspberries contain powerful antioxidants that fight free radicals, reduce inflammation, and inhibit tumor growth. They are a rich source of vitamin C, which supports your immune system, and ellagic acid, a compound that helps fight cancer.

Salad:

- 4 Granny Smith apples
- ½ cup fresh mint (chopped)
- 2 tbsp lemon balm (chopped)- optional
- 8 cups green leaf or red leaf lettuce
- Almond slivers
- Serve with soup or grain of choice

Macerated Raspberry Vinaigrette:

- ½ cup EVOO
- ¼ cup balsamic
- 3-4 crushed raspberries
- Dash of honey

1. Chop the apples.

2. Mix the dressing and add to the chopped apples.

3. Chop mint and lemon balm.

4. In a salad bowl add the lettuce.

5. Add apples to the lettuce and sprinkle with herbs and almonds. Serve immediately with soup or grain of choice.

Arugula Pea Salad with Parmesan and Mint

In the summer, my garden overflows with herbs, so I pop them into every dish to infuse flavor and health benefits.

Mint helps bile secretion to speed up digestion and aids liver health. Peppermint contains a compound called menthol, which can help IBS by relaxing the muscles of the digestive tract.

Can't do Parmesan? Try subbing with hemp seeds for a cheesy flavor reminiscent of pine nuts and that will make this dish vegan.

- 4 cups shelled peas (or frozen)
- 1 dash of sea salt to taste
- 3 tbsp EVOO
- 1 tbsp balsamic vinegar or lemon juice
- 1 dash of freshly ground black pepper to taste
- ½ cup fresh mint leaves (chopped)
- ¼ cup basil (chopped)
- ½ cup shaved Parmesan cheese
- Sourdough bread or bread of choice
- EVOO

1. Bring a large saucepan of water to a boil.
2. Lightly salt the water, then add peas; cover, and simmer for 5-6 minutes until tender.
3. Drain and rinse with cold water, then spread on a towel to dry.
4. Using a medium bowl, whisk together the EVOO, lemon juice, and pepper. Add peas and basil and toss to coat. Let sit for a few minutes to integrate flavor then toss in shaved Parmesan.
5. Toast sourdough bread, drizzle EVOO on the bread.
6. Serve salad with the toasted bread.

Beet Ceviche (V)

Beets contain nutrients that lower blood pressure, fight cancer, and reduce inflammation, boost stamina, and support detoxification by aiding liver health. That means better hormones and metabolism.

Do beets boost athletic performance? Yes! Raw beets raise nitric oxide levels which improves lung function and strengthens muscle contraction.

Betanin, a compound found in beets, shows promise in slowing down the progression of Alzheimer's disease.

Extra virgin olive oil is rich in omega 9 (oleic acid) which boosts the efficacy of your omega 3 intake. Oleic acid has been shown to reduce levels of C-reactive protein (CRP), which is a measure of inflammation. Make sure to include this test in your yearly bloodwork!

Extra virgin olive oil is also a great heart healthy oil to cook with providing your heat does not exceed medium high, or 375 degrees.

- 4 cups raw grated beets
- ½ cup EVOO
- ½ cup lemon juice or balsamic
- ¼ cup fresh dill
- 2 tbsp raw red onions (chopped)

1. Add all the ingredients in a salad bowl and toss. Let sit for 30 minutes and serve.

Blackberry and Fried Goat Cheese Salad

Blackberries are rich in vitamin C and manganese. Like vitamin C, manganese plays a key role in the formation of collagen. Manganese may also help prevent osteoporosis and manage blood sugar levels. Blackberries are also incredibly rich in fiber; 1 cup has 8 grams!

Blackberry Dressing:

- ½ cup blackberries (chopped)
- 2 tbsp balsamic vinegar
- 2 tbsp EVOO
- 2 tbsp honey
- 1 tsp coconut aminos
- 2 large garlic cloves (minced)
- Salt and pepper to taste

Fried Goat Cheese:

- 8 oz. goat cheese, sliced into ¼-inch thick discs
- ¼ cup flour or almond flour
- 1 large egg (lightly beaten)
- 1 cup panko, plus more as needed
- Avocado oil (for frying)

Salad:

- 6 cups lettuce of choice
- 1 cup blackberries
- ½ avocado (sliced)
- ¼ cup red onion (sliced)
- ¼ cup pecans or almonds

Blackberry Dressing:

1. Put all ingredients in a blender or food processor and pulse for 20 seconds until combined and chunky, then store in a cruet.

Fried Goat Cheese:

2. Dredge the goat cheese slices in the flour, coat in egg, followed by panko to form fritters. Let rest for 5 minutes.

3. If fritters feel too wet, dredge though more panko.

4. In a medium skillet add avocado oil and fry fritters over medium high heat, until lightly golden brown. Flip and repeat on uncooked side. Using a slotted spoon remove from skillet and place on towels to drain.

Salad:

5. Place the salad ingredients on a platter, then gently top with fried goat cheese. Drizzle with blackberry vinaigrette. Serve immediately.

Carrot Ginger Soup (V)

Carrot ginger soup is a mainstay of *The Metabolism Plan* and wonderfully anti-inflammatory. The portions used in this recipe, adapted from *The Metabolism Plan*, are for bulk cooking. This allows you to take advantage of those economical 5 pound bags of carrots and to save time by freezing the excess for future use!

Ginger is known to help relieve nausea and gas and help rebalance GI function. Cooking carrots does intensify the sugars. This soup does best after a protein rich breakfast like flax, compote or eggs.

- 1 tbsp cinnamon
- 1 tbsp cumin
- 1 tbsp freshly ground black pepper
- 1 tsp cloves
- 1 tsp cardamom
- 1 tsp sage
- ½ tsp turmeric
- ½ tsp allspice

- 7 quarts water or homemade stock
- 5 lb. carrots (chopped)
- 2 large red onions (chopped)
- 3 large zucchinis (chopped)
- 1 fennel bulb (chopped)
- 8 cloves of garlic
- 3 inches ginger (chopped)

1. Add the cinnamon, cumin, black pepper, cloves, cardamom, sage, turmeric and allspice to a dry skillet and sauté, stirring constantly for 30 seconds. Remove from heat.

2. Add 7 quarts of water or broth to a large soup pot. Add the carrots, onion, zucchini, fennel, garlic, and ginger to the water and then add the toasted spices. Bring the water to a boil and let simmer for 45 minutes until the carrots are soft. Reserve 2 quarts of water for future soup stocks. Blend the carrot soup in batches.

3. Let cool and freeze surplus in mason jars.

Yield: 5 quarts

Carrot Ginger Soup, page 48

Thai Kale Stew, page 66

Carrot Zoodles with Creamy Ginger Dressing, page 50

Carrot Zoodles with Creamy Ginger Dressing (V)

Carrots are rich in beta-carotene, an amazing anti-oxidant which has been shown to have anti-cancer qualities. Diets high in beta-carotene may reduce the risk of lung cancer and colon cancer. A recent study found that carrot juice extract could kill leukemia cells!

If you can't find carrots large enough to spiralize, you can use butternut squash and cook a bit longer than the carrots, say for 4-5 minutes.

Lime Ginger Dressing:

- 2 tbsp raw nut butter
- 4 tbsp coconut milk
- 2 tbsp coconut aminos
- 1 clove garlic (chopped)
- 1 tablespoon ginger (grated)
- 1 tbsp lime juice
- 1 tsp honey
- ½ tsp chipotle

Carrot Zoodles:

- 6 cups spiralized carrots
- 1 tbsp EVOO
- 1 tbsp sesame oil
- 2 tbsp basil (minced)
- 1 tbsp fresh mint (chopped)
- 2 tbsp sesame oil
- 2 tbsp fresh mint
- 2 tbsp fresh basil
- ½ cup peanuts

Lime Ginger Dressing:

1. Combine all the ingredients in a small bowl and mix until smooth and creamy.

Carrot Zoodles:

2. Wash carrots well and pat them dry.

3. Using your spiral slicer, make noodles out of all the carrots, or use a vegetable peeler.

4. In a medium sauté pan over medium heat, add the EVOO and sesame oil. When the pan is hot, add the carrots and sauté for 2-3 minutes. Put the carrots in a large serving bowl. Pour the lime ginger dressing over the noodles, tossing gently.

5. Serve with nuts and freshly chopped mint and basil.

Cream of Broccoli Soup (V)

A protein-rich, delicious, creamy soup that is a family favorite. Feel free to leave out the chilies if you want to tone down the heat.

- 3 tbsp avocado oil
- 1 large onion (chopped)
- 1 tbsp dried sage
- 1 tsp ground cumin
- ½ tsp celery seed
- 4 cups water or Homemade Vegetable Broth (page 58)
- 2 cups water
- 1 can (14 oz) coconut milk
- 8 cups chopped broccoli (from about 4 heads)
- 4 cups chopped zucchini (from about 2 medium)
- 1 small cayenne pepper, or 1 tbsp Sriracha
- 1 medium avocado, peeled and pitted

1. In a medium skillet, add avocado oil over medium heat. Add onion, sage, cumin, and celery seed and sauté until onion is tender.

2. In a medium soup pot, combine sautéed onion, stock, water, coconut milk, broccoli, zucchini, and cayenne pepper or Sriracha. Bring water to a boil and simmer vegetables until tender, about 30 minutes.

3. Transfer soup to blender in batches and blend, adding avocado.

Cream of Kale and Fennel Soup (V)

Kale is not only rich in calcium, it's also a great vegan source of protein and folate and CHOCK full of fiber. It's also a decent source of vegan omega 3. Remember that EVOO can help your body better utilize Omega 3 and help reduce inflammation.

Fennel is anti-inflammatory and rich in vitamin C, potassium, and folate. Fennel is high in fiber which decreases the risk of heart disease and helps to lower cholesterol.

The fats in coconut milk are medium chain triglyceride fats (MCT) and there is some evidence that this may boost weight loss and metabolism. Certainly, consuming enough fat will keep you fuller for a longer period. MCT is unique in that it goes directly from the digestive tract to the liver and is used for energy. Thus, it is less likely to be stored as fat, and instead is used to fuel liver function.

You could add grains or seeds to hit TMP (*The Metabolism Plan*) protein goals for lunch.

- 3 tbsp of EVOO
- 1 large onion (chopped)
- 1 fennel bulb (chopped)
- 1 large zucchini (chopped)
- 10 cups kale (chopped)
- 2 cloves of garlic
- 1 small potato (chopped)
- 3 cups homemade vegetable broth (page 58)
- One can of coconut milk
- Sea salt and pepper to taste.

1. Add the EVOO, chopped onions, fennel, and zucchini in a large stock pot over medium heat. Heat for about 6-8 minutes or until the onions and fennel are soft.

2. Lower the heat and add the kale and 2 cloves of garlic (you can leave it whole if you want because it's going to be blended), and potato.

3. Add the broth and coconut milk and cook for about 15 minutes until the potatoes are soft and the kale is cooked. Add sea salt and pepper to taste

4. Remove from heat and let cool.

5. Add the soup to the food processor to blend.

6. Serve warm or refrigerate.

Cream of Mushroom Soup (V)

Hands down, this is one of my favorite cold-weather comfort soups. Mushrooms are a great source of vitamin D, so very much needed in the cooler weather. Shiitake mushrooms are used for boosting the immune system, lowering cholesterol levels, and diabetes management. It can help reduce eczema flares and fight colds and flu. They are also powerful cancer fighters, specifically breast and prostate cancers.

- 2 tbsp EVOO
- ½ cup leeks, finely chopped
- ½ tsp dried sage
- ¼ tsp sea salt
- Freshly ground black pepper to taste
- 1½ cups diced shiitake and enoki mushrooms (mixed)
- 1 cup homemade vegetable broth (page 58)
- 2 cups canned coconut milk

1. Add the oil and sauté the leeks in a medium skillet over medium heat for 4 minutes.

2. Add the sage, salt, pepper, and mushrooms and cook for an additional minute on medium-low heat, stirring frequently.

3. Add the vegetable broth and reduce the heat, cooking for 5 minutes more. Add the coconut milk and stir for 1 minute. Serve immediately.

Curried Mung Bean Soup (V)

I stuck to the least reactive beans for this cookbook: brown lentils, chickpeas, and pintos. The next bean to test would be mung beans. The warming curry spices aid digestion. The fiber of kale is wonderful for helping to break down the cellulose of beans.

Studies show the high antioxidant in mung beans can neutralize free radical damage specifically to cancer growth in lung and stomach cells. Both lung and stomach cancer are very tough cancers to battle. Sprouted mung beans have six times more antioxidants than regular mung beans. Potassium, fiber and magnesium are all present in good amounts in mung beans. Studies have shown that mung beans can suppress enzymes that naturally raise blood pressure.

- 1½ cups mung beans
- 3 tbsp avocado oil
- 1½ tbsp cumin
- 1 tsp coriander
- ½ tsp turmeric
- ½ tsp cinnamon
- ½ tsp finely grated fresh ginger
- 1 cup onions (diced)
- 3 cloves garlic (minced)
- 1 cup carrots (diced)
- 1 zucchini (chopped)
- 2 cups kale (finely chopped)
- 4 cups vegetable stock
- 1 cup coconut milk (optional)
- 1 tsp fresh ground black pepper
- ½ tsp sea salt

1. Soak the mung beans overnight; drain and rinse when ready to use.

2. Heat the oil in a large saucepan. Add the spices, and toast them in the oil for one minute, then add the onions and garlic and cook for 5 minutes.

3. Add the remaining ingredients, simmering until the beans are tender, for about 45 minutes.

4. Serve warm with salad of choice.

Delicata Kale Salad (V)

Did you know that delicata is the least reactive of all the winter squashes? It's not always the easiest to find, but it's worth it! Just like with your kids, it's hard to choose a favorite but, boy, is delicata up there. The sweetness of the delicata squash stands up nicely to the kale, and the colors combine so beautifully.

To make this vegan lunch protein perfect, you can add a grain like wild rice, hemp seeds or pumpkin seeds. .

- 2 tbsp EVOO
- 1 medium delicata squash, cut into ½-inch cubes
- ¼ cup rice cooking wine
- 4 cups kale (deveined and chopped)
- 1 cup pomegranate arils
- 1 green apple (chopped)
- Wild rice, hemp seeds or pumpkin seeds (optional)

1. Heat the oil in a medium skillet.

2. Add the squash and sauté for 1 minute.

3. Add the rice wine and cover skillet for 5 minutes or until the squash is tender.

4. Add the kale and sauté for 1 additional minute, with the cover off, until the kale starts to wilt.

5. Remove from heat and place in bowl. Top with pomegranate, chopped green apple, and additional protein sources for a lunch option.

French Onion Lentil Soup (V)

This is a mashup of French onion soup and lentil stew with amazing protein levels-enough for a TMP dinner. So, for you folks looking to boost protein to fuel your workouts, look no further.

French lentils are rich in fiber, which helps regulate glucose levels and lower cholesterol. What's the difference between regular lentils and French lentils? Glad you asked. French lentils are closer to green lentils but darker and 1/3rd the size. What makes them great for dishes is they don't turn into a mushy texture and hold their shape really well. This makes it especially good for salads. They also take slightly less time to cook.

Bay leaves aid digestion, are cancer fighting and help to fight anxiety and stress. Research has shown that ground bay leaves can act much like cinnamon does, taking it before a meal can lead to better blood sugar.

I encourage you to try and mix and match all these recipes but do note that beans and rice in the same meal tends to be higher inflammatory. Beans and broccoli in the same meal tends to promote gas which can impair digestion, healing and optimal weight loss.

- 3 tbsp EVOO
- 2 onions (thinly sliced)
- 2 cloves of garlic (chopped)
- 1 cup red wine
- 2-3 cups homemade vegetable broth (page 58) or water
- 1 cup French lentils rinsed
- 2 bay leaves
- 1 tbsp fresh thyme (chopped)
- Sea salt and pepper
- Salad of choice

1. Heat a medium-sized soup pot over medium-high heat and add the EVOO. Add the onions and cook over a low heat for 20 minutes, stirring frequently until softened.

2. Stir in the garlic, cooking for 30 seconds; add the wine, and 2 cups of vegetable broth.

3. Bring the mix to a boil and then stir in the lentils, bay leaves, and thyme and season with salt and pepper.

4. Reduce to a simmer for 30 minutes, adding more broth toward the end of the cooking to keep the lentils in liquid. Once the lentils are tender, remove the bay leaves.

5. Serve warm with a salad of choice.

Frisée "Lardons" with Mushroom "Bacon" (DF)

I practically grew up working in French restaurants, so to turn this classic bistro salad into a vegetarian dish was super fun. Frisée is rich in vitamins A, K, and B. It's also high in manganese and helps regulate blood sugar, carbohydrate metabolism, calcium absorption, and fighting free radicals.

- 1 cup mushroom bacon (see page 131)
- 2 heads frisée
- ¼ cup vinegar
- 4 eggs

- Vinaigrette of choice
- Sea salt and pepper
- Salad or soup of choice

1. Prepare mushroom bacon.

2. Wash and dry the frisée and place in a shallow salad bowl.

3. Using a medium-sized pot, add two-thirds water along with vinegar. Bring to a gentle simmer. Crack each egg into a cup, carefully lowering them into the water. Poach the eggs for 3-4 minutes until the whites have set, with the yolks still soft. With a slotted spoon, remove and let drain on a towel

4. Toss the frisée with vinaigrette. Divide the frisée between 2 plates, placing the egg in the center of each. Sprinkle the warm mushroom bacon over the salad. Add freshly ground black pepper and serve.

Grilled Caesar Salad

Romaine hearts are difficult to digest. Have you ever noticed how bloated you can feel after a salad? Grilling them makes it easier for your body to process. If you don't have a grill you can broil for 2-3 minutes. In winter, I also love to do a quick sauté to wilt the leaves for a quick, easy stir-fried green.

- 2 romaine hearts
- EVOO for grilling
- Sea salt and pepper

- Plan Caesar dressing (see page 133)

1. Heat the barbecue or broiler to medium to medium-high heat.

2. Cut the romaine heart(s) in half lengthwise. Brush the cut sides with EVOO, then sprinkle with salt and pepper.

3. Serve the romaine hearts whole with dressing. Serve with a protein rich soup or warm grain.

Homemade Vegetable Broth (V)

I am always dismayed by how many "good quality" low-sodium stocks will have MSG or alternative forms of MSG, like yeast extract or autolyzed yeast which is rich in glutamate. You see, for sensitive folks like me, this can act like MSG and not only cause major weight gain, but also serious issues like headaches, migraines, sinus infections, and heart palpitations. MSG has been linked to health issues like Alzheimer's and Parkinson's.

Celery tends to be higher reactive, so I use celery seeds in my soups instead to bump up the flavor. Celery seeds are a natural diuretic, can lower blood pressure and reduce arthritic pain and gout. It is also good for muscle cramps. It has a long tradition in Ayurvedic medicine for improving heart health.

Making your own stock is super easy. You can use your leftover vegetable scraps, saving on money, protecting the environment and preventing waste.

- 1 tbsp EVOO
- 5 cloves garlic (minced)
- 2 large onions (chopped)
- 3 carrots (chopped)
- 8 cups water
- 2 cups vegetable scraps (think fennel, carrot ends, tomato, leeks, onion)
- 2 bay leaves
- A few sprigs of dill, tarragon, and thyme
- 1 tsp celery seeds
- 1 tsp sage
- Sea salt and pepper to taste

1. Heat the EVOO and garlic in a large stock pot over medium heat.
2. Add the onions and cook for 10 minutes over a low heat until they are browned.
3. Add the rest of the ingredients and simmer for 45 minutes.
4. Pour the broth through a fine mesh strainer into a large heat-proof bowl or pot; discard solids. Season with salt and pepper.
5. Once the broth has cooled, transfer it to containers, and store it in the freezer for use as needed.

Italian Chickpea Soup (V)

Stewing canned chickpeas is definitely the best way to make them easier to digest. The extra stewing time helps to break down the cellulose. It's when we can't digest a food that we are unable to properly assimilate the nutrients, but also inhibit weight loss. That can be demoralizing when you are working so hard to eat healthy, right? But simple tweaks can go a long way for best health and best weight.

- 1 tbsp EVOO
- 1 onion (finely chopped)
- 2 cloves of garlic (minced)
- 2 carrots (chopped)
- 1 fennel bulb (cut into thin slices)
- 2 cans low-sodium chickpeas
- 2 cups low-reactive tomato sauce (page 131)
- 3 cups vegetable broth
- ½ tsp celery seeds

- 4 cups lactino kale (deveined and chopped)
- 1 zucchini spiralized
- 1 tsp dried oregano
- ½ tsp dried thyme
- Black pepper to taste
- Hemp seeds or protein of choice
- Fresh basil chopped

1. Heat the EVOO and sauté the onion for about 3 minutes in a large pot, then add the garlic, carrots, and fennel. Cook for about 4 minutes.

2. Stir in the chickpeas, tomato sauce, vegetable broth, and celery seeds. Cook for about 15 minutes, then add the kale, zucchini, herbs, and pepper and cook for another 6-8 minutes.

3. Top each serving with 1-2 tbsp of hemp seeds and fresh basil. Serve immediately.

Italian Chickpea Soup, page 59

Pumpkin Seed Hummus, page

Italian Vegetable and Tomato Soup

Spinach is a good source of protein. Cooking it helps to make the high iron content more bioavailable and helps deactivate the goitrogens a bit. Spinach is also high in magnesium which helps to regulate mood and deep sleep. Its high potassium content can help lower blood pressure and exercise recovery.

When you purchase tomato sauce, try to buy a sauce that is citric acid free. Most citric acid is artificially prepared. It is produced from a mold, and even though this is filtered out, it can still affect people who suffer from mold allergies, Lyme disease, depression, migraines and auto-immune issues.

- 1 tbsp EVOO
- 1 onion (finely chopped)
- 2 cloves of garlic (minced)
- 2 carrots (cut into medium-sized chunks)
- 1 yellow squash (chopped
- 1 fennel bulb (cut into thin slices)
- 2 cups low-reactive tomato sauce (page 131)
- 6 cups vegetable broth
- ½ tsp celery seed
- 8 cups fresh spinach
- 1 tsp dried oregano
- ½ tsp dried thyme
- 1 tbsp fresh basil (chopped)
- black pepper to taste
- 4 pieces sourdough bread or bread or choice
- EVOO
- ½ cup grated Parmesan or cheese of choice

1. Heat the EVOO and sauté the onion for about 3 minutes in a large pot, then add the garlic, carrots, squash, and fennel. Cook for about 4 minutes.

2. Stir in the tomato sauce, vegetable broth, and celery seed. Cook for about 15 minutes, then add the spinach, herbs, and pepper. Cook for another 2-3 minutes.

3. Put the broiler on high and brush the bread with EVOO. Divide the cheese into 4 portions, sprinkling it on the bread. Broil the bread until the cheese is lightly browned. Enjoy immediately with the soup.

Persian Barley Soup (Ash-e Jo) (V)

Barley is a rich source of iron, zinc, and selenium, which is a mineral that supports thyroid health. Selenium also helps to reduce the cellular damage from free radicals thereby lowering risk of disease. Research has shown that barley is one of the best grains for aiding balanced blood sugar and lowered cholesterol.

Persian cuisine is very lavish in its use of herbs which not only impacts dishes from a culinary standpoint but also from a health promoting aspect.

You can purchase advieh in Middle Eastern stores or use the recipe on page120.

- 1 onion (diced)
- 3 tbsp EVOO
- 1 tsp advieh
- ¼ tsp celery seed
- 4 cups vegetable stock
- 2 cups water
- 1 cup pearled barley
- 1 large carrot
- 2 cups kale (chopped)
- 1 cup coconut milk
- Sea salt and pepper to taste
- 1 lime
- 1 teaspoon chopped parsley for garnish

1. Heat the oil in a large pot, and sauté the onions, advieh and celery seed on medium-low heat until translucent (about 6–8 minutes).

2. Add the broth and one cup of water, along with the barley, and simmer on low.

3. Continue to simmer for about 90 minutes, adding more water or broth as needed.

4. Chop the carrots and add the kale with the coconut milk to the barley. Cook for 5 minutes.

5. Season to taste with sea salt, pepper, and lime. Garnish with parsley.

6. Serve warm.

Potato Kale Chowder (V)

Potatoes, potatoes, how I love thee! A medium potato has 900 mg of potassium and is a good source of fiber and B6. They are also a moderate source of protein, and oh so hearty and satisfying.

Tarragon is a natural diuretic and aids digestion. It's also used to fight cancer, aid heart health and balance blood sugar. Tarragon is a sleep aid and can help to regulate hormones. It also aids gut health for better absorption of nutrients, immune function and mood.

Potatoes and kale are both great vegan protein sources, so you wouldn't need to add much to make this a perfect protein lunch. But I must admit, I love this soup with a chapati topped with pesto.

- 5 tbsp avocado oil
- 1 large yellow onion (chopped)
- 2 garlic cloves chopped
- 4 large potatoes (chopped)
- 6 cups vegetable broth (page 58)
- 6 cups chopped kale (deveined)
- 2 cups coconut milk
- 1 tsp tarragon
- 1 tsp thyme
- ¼ tsp celery seed
- sea salt to taste
- freshly ground black pepper
- optional: cayenne to taste

1. Heat the avocado oil in a large pot over medium-high heat. Add the onions, garlic and potatoes and sauté until golden brown for 5–8 minutes. Add the broth, kale and coconut milk and herbs; simmer for 7–10 minutes until the kale is soft. Stir occasionally.

2. Season with sea salt, fresh ground pepper, and optional cayenne.

Potato Salad (V)

So delish! Vegan potato salad. By now, you might have figured out that I'm a potato FANATIC. I'm also highly reactive to eggs, so I can't do mayonnaise. The avocado "mayo" makes this dish creamy and boosts potassium. A medium potato has roughly 5 grams of protein, so you would use this salad as a side dish for your lunch or dinner. Red potatoes are lower in starch, other lower starch options are fingerlings and Yukon Gold potatoes.

Raw red onions can be a bit higher reactive but combining them with avocado reduces the reactivity. Onions are high in sulfur which supports the body's natural ability to detox. Sulfur is one of the best chelating agents and helps to bind heavy metals and flush them from your body.

- 8 red potatoes (chopped)
- 1 cup fennel (chopped)
- ½ tsp celery seed
- ½ tsp garlic powder
- ½ cup avocado mayo (page 121)
- Sea salt and black pepper to taste
- 2 tbsp chopped red onion (optional)
- 1 tbsp chopped chives (optional)
- Radicchio, frisée, or endive (chopped)
- Fresh basil

1. Place the potatoes and fennel in a medium pot with boiling water and simmer for 8–10 minutes until both are soft to the touch.

2. Remove from heat and rinse under cold water.

3. Add celery seed, garlic powder, and avocado mayo and mix well. Season with sea salt and black pepper.

4. Add optional red onion or chives as desired.

5. Serve potatoes on salad of choice and garnish with basil.

Provencal Leek Soup (DF)

Like spinach, swiss chard is a goitrogen, so limit this amazing soup to once a week or substitute kale for the chard. Swiss chard can help regulate blood sugar and boost immune function. It's also a good vegan source of calcium. One cup of swiss chard has three times the daily requirement of vitamin K, making it excellent for bone health. It can help to combat cancer and reduce blood pressure. Swiss chard is rich in alpha lipoic acid which may help to prevent damage from a stroke. It is also a good source in chlorophyll which can help to offset the cancer-causing chemicals that are produced when grilling meat. So, make sure to include swiss chard at your next barbecue.

Eggs and grains tend to be a higher reactive food combination for most, so you could boost the protein and keep this dairy free by adding in some seeds or nuts to a salad.

- 2 tbsp EVOO
- 2 leeks (cut in half lengthwise, sliced, rinsed of dirt, and drained on paper towel)
- 4 garlic cloves (chopped)
- ½ sea salt plus more to taste
- 6 cups chopped Swiss chard or kale
- 8 cups Homemade Broth (page 58)
- Black pepper to taste
- 4 large eggs

1. Heat 1 tbsp of EVOO in a large soup pot over medium heat and add the leeks. Cook, stirring until tender, for 3-5 minutes.

2. Add the garlic and ½ teaspoon of salt, and cook, stirring until the garlic is fragrant, for about 1 minute.

3. Add the greens and stir until they begin to wilt. Add broth and bring to a simmer, partially covered, for 15-20 minutes until the greens are very tender. Add pepper, taste, and adjust seasoning.

4. Beat the eggs in a bowl.

5. Add a cup of the soup to the eggs in the bowl and stir. Afterwards, add the egg mixture to the remaining soup.

6. Simmer for 1-2 minutes. Serve immediately.

Thai Butternut Squash Stew (V)

Just one cup of butternut squash has 500 mg of potassium and 7 g of fiber! It's also very rich in vitamin A, lutein, and zeaxanthin, which are all important nutrients for eye health. Butternut is rich in beta carotene which is a powerful antioxidant that lowers risks of respiratory aliments. Studies found that those who consume high beta-carotene food sources are less likely to have asthma attacks.

Basil has a long tradition of use in Ayurvedic medicine. Basil fights free radicals thus slowing the aging process. Basil contains essential oils that help lower inflammation. The essential oils are powerfully antibacterial and antiviral and can help provide resistance to infections.

- 1 tbsp sesame oil
- 2 garlic cloves (minced or grated)
- 1-inch fresh ginger (grated)
- 1 red chili pepper (chopped)
- 2 scallions (chopped)
- 3½ cups homemade broth (58)
- 6 cups butternut (chopped into cubes)
- 1 tbsp rounded creamy peanut butter or almond butter
- 2 tbsp coconut aminos
- 1 (15 ounce) can coconut milk
- 2 cups zucchini noodles
- 1 tbsp chopped tarragon
- 1 tsp fresh basil (chopped)

1. Heat a soup pot over medium heat and add the sesame oil. Immediately add the garlic, ginger, chili pepper, and scallions. Cook for 1 minute or until fragrant.

2. Slowly stir in the broth, then add the butternut. Bring the soup to a boil and simmer for 15 minutes.

3. Add the peanut butter, coconut aminos, and coconut milk, stirring to combine. Add the zucchini noodles and tarragon, cooking until tender for about 6-8 minutes.

4. Ladle the soup into bowls and garnish with basil. Serve immediately.

Thai Kale Stew (V)

This stew is a great starting point to add additional proteins, whether served with beans, grains, or seeds. Zucchini and yellow squash are high in potassium, making them natural diuretics. Potassium is an essential electrolyte, so it's also super important for muscle function.

Coriander helps to maintain balanced blood sugar, cholesterol and blood pressure.

Tomatoes are rich in lycopene which can combat prostate cancer and are also rich in folate which can help to break down homocysteine. High levels of homocysteine have been associated with greater risk of heart attacks.

- 2 tbsp red Thai curry paste
- 4 cups homemade vegetable stock (page 58) or water
- 1 leek (rinsed and chopped)
- 1 red onion (chopped)
- 2 garlic cloves (chopped)
- 1 tbsp ginger (fine grated)
- 1 tsp coconut aminos
- 1 tsp coriander
- 3 yellow squash (diced)
- ½ cup low-reactive tomato sauce (page 131)
- 1 cup full-fat coconut milk
- 1 tbsp agave
- 2 large zucchinis (spiralized)
- 2 carrots (chopped)
- 8 cups of kale (finely chopped)
- 4 shiitake (chopped)
- Sea salt and freshly ground black pepper to taste
- Spicy roasted sunflower seeds (page 104) for garnish

1. Heat the red Thai curry paste with ½ cup vegetable stock in a large pot over medium-high heat. Add the chopped leeks, onion, garlic, ginger, coconut aminos, and coriander and sauté, stirring frequently, for 5 minutes. Add the squash and another cup of vegetable stock. Continue to sauté for an additional 5 minutes.

2. Stir in the remaining vegetable stock, low-reactive tomato sauce, coconut milk, agave, vegetables, mushrooms, salt, and pepper and simmer for 30 minutes.

3. Top with spicy sunflower seeds and serve warm.

Vietnamese Mango and Cashew Salad (V)

Ok, I'll admit it. I love spicy food. This salad is so much more than a spicy treat though. It is a powerful weight loss and cancer fighting dish. Research has shown that mangoes protect against breast, prostate, and colon cancer.

Food scientist Heidi Allen states that you can lose 10 times as much weight if you add some chili to your meals. Red chilis have higher antioxidant properties than the green chilis. Chilis are also rich in capsaicin. Capsaicin has been shown to effectively combat prostate cancer. Also, according to recent studies, may help to fight breast cancer stem cells and help to decrease tumors in lung cancer. Capsaicin is also a powerful pain reliever, and helpful for joint and arthritic pain.

Cashews are packed with vitamins like E, K, and B6, along with minerals like copper, phosphorus, zinc, magnesium, iron, and selenium. The copper and iron in cashews help the body form and utilize red blood cells. The high copper content in cashew nuts helps fight against cancerous cells. It also helps the body form collagen and absorb iron. Low copper levels can lead to graying hair, as well as fatigue, bruising easily, and always feeling cold. It is speculated that low copper levels also contribute to arthritis which is why you may see people wearing copper bracelets.

Dressing

- $\frac{1}{3}$ cup lime juice
- 2 tbsp agave or honey
- 2 tsp fresh ginger (grated)
- 1 tbsp coconut aminos
- 1 tbsp toasted sesame oil

Salad

- 2 slightly under-ripe mangos (cut into medium sticks)
- ½ red onion (cut into thin rings & soaked in cold water)
- 1 small Vietnamese chili
- ¼ cup fresh mint (finely chopped)
- ¼ cup basil (finely chopped)
- 6 cups lightly sautéed kale
- ½ cup chopped cashew nuts

1. Place the lime juice, agave, ginger, aminos, and sesame oil in a medium-sized bowl.
2. Combine the dressing with the mango, red onion, chili, and herbs.
3. Add the kale to the bowl, mix well and garnish with cashews.

Warm Broccoli & Potato Salad with Apple Vinaigrette

This is another perfect high protein lunch thanks to potatoes, broccoli and pecans. Pecans are a rich source of vitamin E, which protect your cells from damage and helps maintain skin health and a glowing complexion. Pecans are rich in oleic acid which has shown to kill breast cancer cells in studies. They also contains phosphorus which is one of the most abundant minerals in the body. Phosphorus also helps to prevent DOMS (delayed onset muscle soreness), so you can reap better benefits from your workouts.

Pecans are also a good source of magnesium which is known for its anti-inflammatory benefits and mood boosting capabilities. Magnesium can help to lower inflammatory markers like C-reactive protein. It can also reduce inflammation in the arterial walls, thus reducing the risk of heart disease, strokes, arthritis, and Alzheimer's disease.

- 2 cups water or homemade vegetable broth (page 58)
- 1 lb. red potatoes (chopped)
- 2 bunches broccoli (chopped)
- ½ cup pecan halves
- 3 tbsp EVOO
- 1 apple (chopped)
- 2 tbsp balsamic vinegar
- 1 garlic clove(chopped)
- ½ tsp fresh thyme
- ½ tsp fresh black pepper
- ½ tsp sea salt
- 4 ounces Manchego, grated

1. Fill a medium pot with 2 cups of water or vegetable broth.

2. Add the chopped potatoes and cook over medium heat. Add the broccoli after 5 minutes and simmer for another 5 minutes.

3. Drain the broccoli and potatoes in a colander.

4. Using a small skillet, dry toast the pecans over medium heat for 1 minute.

5. Remove pecans and set aside.

6. Lower the heat on the skillet and add EVOO, apple, vinegar, garlic, thyme, black pepper, and sea salt. Simmer apple vinaigrette for 1-2 minutes.

7. Add the broccoli and potatoes in a salad bowl; drizzle with apple vinaigrette; and top with Manchego and pecans.

8. Serve with your salad of choice or enjoy as a side dish.

Warm Salad Tre Colori

The bitter greens in this dish are amazing for gall bladder and liver health. Your liver is responsible for over 500 functions (which includes metabolism and hormonal function), so play nice, and try this salad!

Radicchio is a great source of inulin which allows you to better absorb and utilize probiotics. Inulin is also known to activate pancreatic juices, which aid digestion and help maintain balanced blood sugar. It also promotes bile production that supports gall blander health.

Wilting a salad can help to prevent bloating and make absorption of nutrients more available.

- 2 tbsp EVOO
- 2 garlic cloves (finely minced)
- 2 spears endive (washed, dried, and coarsely chopped)
- 1 small radicchio (washed, dried, and coarsely chopped)
- 5 oz. baby arugula (washed, dried, and chopped)
- Vinaigrette of choice
- ½ cup shaved or grated parmesan
- Fresh black pepper
- Bread or soup of choice

1. In a medium skillet, add the EVOO and garlic and cook for 1 minute over medium heat. Add the endive and radicchio and toss for 1-2 minutes until the lettuce is slightly wilted.

2. Add the arugula to a salad bowl and top with the wilted endive and radicchio.

3. Add the vinaigrette and toss for 30 seconds; top with cheese and fresh black pepper.

4. Serve salad warm with bread or soup of choice.

Warm Thai Vegan Salad (V)

A warm and spicy vegan salad, perfect to warm you up on a chilly day. Mangoes are rich in vitamins A, C, and E to support your immune system. So many of us are exposed to hours of blue light which can negatively affect our vision. Mangoes are rich in the antioxidant zeaxanthin, which can negate the harm caused by blue light rays.

Green leaf lettuce is also rich in zeaxanthin, making this a great salad for all of us stuck hours sitting behind a computer!

- 1½ lb. kale
- ½ lb. butternut squash (cut into matchsticks)
- 1 red onion (diced)
- 1 tbsp EVOO
- 1 tbsp sesame oil
- 2 tbsp coconut aminos
- ½ cup peanut butter or raw almond butter
- 2 tbsp lime juice
- 1-2 tbsp red or green Thai curry paste
- ¼ cup water
- 1 tbsp honey
- 1 head red or green leaf lettuce (shredded)
- 1 mango (sliced into matchsticks)
- 1 red Thai chili (thinly sliced)
- ¼ cup chopped roasted peanuts or almond slivers

1. Toss together the first 6 ingredients (kale, butternut, onion, EVOO, sesame oil, coconut aminos) in a medium skillet and sauté for 10–12 minutes. Remove from heat.

2. Using a medium bowl or blender, whisk together the peanut butter, lime juice, curry paste, water, and honey until smooth.

3. Place the lettuce in a bowl and top with sautéed vegetables and mango slivers.

4. Drizzle the salad with peanut sauce and sprinkle with chili and nuts.

Wild Rice Vegetable Stew

This hearty soup is a moderate source of protein, thanks to the wild rice. Shiitakes are a nice source of vitamin D, which helps to regulate hormones.

Rosemary is rich in antioxidants and anti-inflammatory. It is excellent for preventing headaches, enhancing memory, and improving concentration. Rosemary is being researched as an aid for fighting Alzheimer's. Studies indicate that rosemary extract may prevent cancer cells from replicating, which prevents tumor growth. One study found that rosemary (alone or in combination with turmeric) helped to heal estrogen dominant breast cancer.

- 2 cups water
- 1 cup wild rice
- ½ tsp salt
- EVOO for sautéing
- 1 large yellow onion (diced)
- 1 lb. carrots (chopped)
- 1 fennel bulb (chopped)
- ½ lb. shitake mushrooms (diced)
- 1 tsp sage
- 2 garlic cloves (minced)
- 1 tsp oregano
- 1 cup white wine
- 4 cups homemade vegetable stock (page 58)
- 2 tsp fresh rosemary (minced)
- 1 cup coconut milk
- ¼ cup grated cheese of choice
- sautéed greens, such as kale, for garnish

1. Bring a pot of the water to a boil. Add the wild rice and ½ tsp of salt and reduce to a simmer. Cook for 45 minutes or until the rice is tender.

2. While the rice cooks, prepare the rest of the soup. Warm a tbsp of oil in a soup pot over medium-high heat, add the onions, carrots, and fennel, and cook until the onions have softened and turned translucent (6 minutes). Turn the heat down to medium, stir in the mushrooms, and add the sage. Cook for another 10–12 minutes until the mushrooms have released their jus.

3. Add garlic and oregano, and cook until fragrant for about 30 seconds. Increase the heat again to medium-high and pour in the wine. Stir thoroughly. Simmer until the liquid has reduced by roughly half.

4. Add the stock, bring to a boil, and then reduce to a simmer. Simmer for 20 minutes to meld the flavors. Add the rosemary, coconut, and cooked wild rice. Simmer for another 5 minutes. Top with cheese and greens of choice.

Lunches and Appetizers

African Peanut Stew (V)

I remember the first time I had this dish. I was 10 visiting a cultural center, and I instantly fell in love with it. This stew was a big part of my early vegetarian days, and I hope you enjoy it as much as I still do 40+ years later.

Peanuts are not actually nuts, but legumes, so they are closely related to beans like lentils and soy. Peanuts are linked to reduced cardiovascular risk and may also help lower blood pressure. Peanuts are rich in biotin which is important for healthy hair and nails. They are also rich in niacin (B3) which is important for heart health. They also are a goitrogen, so use in moderation.

Traditionally in Asian countries, cumin has been used to help with digestion, coughs, pain, and liver health. In Iran, people use cumin to treat seizures and in India to prevent gas and aid digestion. It may also greatly help with weight loss! One study showed that after 8 weeks one group lost significant weight compared to a group that had a placebo. They also had a decrease in their insulin levels and cholesterol. Additional research indicates cumin may also help to relieve the symptoms of IBS.

- 1 tbsp avocado oil
- 4 garlic cloves (minced)
- 1-inch fresh ginger (finely grated)
- 1 medium onion (chopped)
- 1 lb. butternut squash (diced)
- 1 tsp cumin
- ¼ tsp cayenne

- 2 cups low-reactive tomato sauce (page 131)
- ½ cup chunky peanut butter
- 6 cups vegetable broth
- ½ bunch or 2-3 cups chopped collard greens or kale
- Optional- hearty grain of choice

1. Using a medium-sized pot, add avocado oil. Sauté the garlic and ginger over medium-low heat for 1-2 minutes or until the garlic becomes fragrant.

2. Add onion and continue to sauté for 2-3 minutes. Then add the butternut squash, cumin and cayenne and continue to sauté for 4-5 minutes more.

3. Add the tomato sauce, peanut butter, and broth and stir until everything is evenly mixed. Place a lid on the pot, and then lower heat to simmer. Next add the collards to the soup pot.

4. Cook for about 15 minutes, stirring occasionally.

5. Serve the stew warm. Optional serve with a hearty grain.

Avocado Fries with Sweet and Spicy Dipping Sauce (DF)

Fried avocados are as delicious as you imagine them to be! You can make this in big batches, freeze, and fry later for your dinner or sports parties.

Egg whites are rich in vitamins B2, D, B6, and B1 as well as minerals like selenium, zinc, iron, and copper. If you can't have gluten, you can make this dish with gluten-free panko or almond flour.

Avocados are a great source of vitamins C, E, K, and B-6, as well as riboflavin, niacin, pantothenic acid, magnesium, potassium, and omega-3 fatty acids. While fish oil supplements continue to be of questionable efficacy, there is no doubt that eating foods that are high in omega 3 help to reduce inflammation and boost mood.

Avocados are also rich in folate. Low folate levels are associated with depression and increased risk of many cancers such as colon, lung, pancreatic, cervical and breast.

Avocados are full of healthy fats that keep you satiated. When you eat enough fat, your brain turns off the hunger switch which is why they can be such a great tool for weight loss. Eating fat also slows down the absorption of sugar and carbohydrates.

- 2 firm, ripe avocados
- ½ cup all-purpose flour
- 2 egg whites, beaten
- ½ tbsp melted butter
- 1½ cups panko
- 1 tsp garlic powder
- ½ tsp chipotle powder
- 1 tsp onion powder
- 2 tbsp EVOO for oiling the baking pan
- ½ cup sweet & sour dipping sauce (page 137)

1. Preheat oven to 425 °F.
2. Slice the avocados into 10 slices and set aside.
3. Set out three bowls: place the flour in the first bowl, the egg in the second, and in the third bowl, combine the panko, garlic powder, chipotle and onion powder.
4. Coat each avocado slice in flour, egg, and then panko mix. Place avocado fries on a well-oiled baking pan.
5. Bake for 20 minutes until the fries are browned.

Baked Brie with Fig

This is the easiest appetizer to make for a dinner party. What is not to love about warm, gooey, melted cheese?

Figs are rich in soluble fiber, which keeps you full longer and helps to relieve constipation.

Raw honey helps fight allergies (especially if you buy locally grown) and is rich in antioxidants. Research shows that honey may help digestive disorders such as ulcers. It's also anti-bacterial and anti-fungal because the bees add an enzyme that makes hydrogen peroxide! Honey, particularly buckwheat honey, also helps with coughs. Studies have shown that honey can be as effective as cough syrup with children. Do note that honey should not be given to children under one year old.

- 2 tbsp fig spread
- ¼ cup almond slivers
- 8-ounce wheel of goat Brie
- Avocado oil for pan
- Raw honey (for drizzling)
- Bread or crackers of choice
- 2 fresh figs sliced

1. Preheat oven to 350 °F.
2. Mix the fig spread and almond slivers in a bowl until well combined.
3. Oil skillet and place the wheel of brie in the center.
4. Coat the top of the cheese with the fig-almond spread and bake for 15 minutes.
5. Drizzle with honey and serve with sourdough bread and fig slices.

Caramelized Butternut Squash with Sage Pesto (V)

Butternut squash is one of the easiest winter squashes to pass; it's one of the least reactive, right there after delicata squash. Kombucha squash tends to be more reactive.

Sage is an amazing herb for hot flashes, bronchial issues and allergies. We often simmer sage to steam our faces at my house in winter season to help fight the sniffles and reduce congestion.

This dish is a wonderful addition to your fall and winter arsenal to fight the common cold. Manuka honey helps fight oral bacteria which can boost immune function. It can lower inflammation, is antiviral and antibacterial, and helps fight sore throats and coughs. Studies show it may even help digestive disorders.

As butternut is higher in starch, this side dish would go well with a lower starch vegetable like broccoli or kale to boost protein.

- 2 butternut squashes (about 3 lbs. total; chopped with skin into 1-inch wedges)
- 2 tbsp avocado oil
- 2 tsp Manuka honey
- ¼-½ tsp cayenne to taste
- ½ cup sage pesto (page 128)
- Sea salt and pepper to taste

1. Preheat the oven to 400 °F and place a rack in the middle slot in the oven.
2. Toss the squash with avocado oil, honey and cayenne and place in a single layer on the baking sheet. Bake for 15 minutes. Remove from the oven and flip over. Bake for another 20-25 minutes until browned on the other side and cooked through.
3. Once the squash is roasted, place in the bowl and toss with pesto. Add salt and pepper. Serve immediately.

Cavolo Nero with Roasted Vegetables and Pesto (V)

Cavolo nero, also known as dinosaur kale or lactino kale, is a nice change to green curly-leaf kale, and still has amazing health benefits. It is native to Italy and much research has been conducted there on its healing properties. Cavolo nero contains compounds that are precursors to isothiocyanates. Studies have shown the healing properties of isothiocyanates ranging from fighting cancer to suppression of the growth of tumors. It can also reduce DNA damage. This makes it a strong anti-aging food to add to your arsenal. Like all kale, cavolo nero is a good vegan source of protein. While many people like their kale deveined and chopped, I eat the whole vegetable for its hearty appeal.

Roasting vegetables:

- 6 carrots (chopped)
- 2 cups red onion (chopped)
- 1 zucchini (chopped)
- 1 yellow squash (chopped)
- 3 tbsp EVOO
- 2 garlic cloves (chopped)
- 1 tsp dried basil
- ½ tsp dried rosemary
- ½ tsp oregano

Cavolo Nero:

- 8 cups cavolo nero (deveined and chopped)
- ½ cup water or veg stock
- Pesto of choice
- Optional: grain of choice

1. Preheat the oven to 375 °F and coat the roasting vegetables in 3 tablespoons of EVOO, garlic, and herbs. Roast for 40 minutes. When tender, add to a medium salad bowl.

2. Steam sauté the cavolo nero in water or stock for 5 minutes in a medium skillet with a lid.

3. Remove the cavolo nero with a slotted spoon and add to the roast vegetables.

4. Mix and top with pesto of choice. Optionally, add grain of choice.

Chard and Squash Mole (V)

Chocolate is one of the richest sources of polyphenols. Polyphenols have been linked to numerous health benefits, including reduced inflammation, better blood flow, lower blood pressure, improved cholesterol and lower blood sugar levels. Chocolate is especially abundant in flavanols, which have potent antioxidant and anti-inflammatory effects. Raw cacao powder has nearly four times the antioxidant power of your average chocolate and more than 20 times that of blueberries.

- 4 tbsp EVOO (divided)
- 4 cloves garlic (minced)
- ½ onion (diced)
- 1 tsp agave or honey
- 1 tsp sea salt
- 4 chipotles in adobo
- 1 cup pumpkin seeds (dry toasted in a skillet for one minute)
- ¼ cup raw cocoa powder
- 1 tsp cumin
- 1 tsp cinnamon
- ½ tsp allspice
- 5 cups vegetable broth
- 1 tbsp oregano (preferably Mexican oregano)
- 8 cups Swiss chard (finely chopped)
- 2 yellow squashes (chopped)
- 1 zucchini (chopped)
- 1 carrot (chopped)
- Grain of choice

1. For the mole sauce, heat 2 tbsp of the EVOO oil in a medium-sized saucepan over medium heat.

2. Add the garlic, onion and agave, and cook until the onion has softened approx. 5-6 minutes.

3. Add the salt, chipotle, pumpkin seeds, cocoa powder, cumin, cinnamon, allspice, 4 cups of the vegetable broth, and oregano and bring to a simmer. Cook for about 20 minutes.

4. Remove from heat; transfer to a blender; purée; then return to the saucepan. Keep on simmer as you prepare your vegetables.

5. Using a skillet, add 2 tbsp of the EVOO, then add vegetables. Stir until well coated with oil, then add 1 cup of the vegetable broth. Cover and let simmer for 10 minutes until tender.

6. Remove the cover and stir until most of the broth has evaporated.

7. Mix the vegetables with the mole and serve on a bed of grain of choice.

Cheesylicious Mushroom Kale Queso

Cheesylicious Queso – spicy or not, you choose! Shiitakes are cancer-fighters and support immune function.

The fiber in kale aids digestion.

Onions are a rich source of sulfur which aids detoxification and helps to heal mucosa (sinuses, lungs, gut health). The sulfur compounds in red onions also lower bad cholesterol. Sulfur improves cell membrane function and aids fat metabolism. This dish was made for your brunches and sports parties. To boost protein even more you could add the Ranchero Pinto Beans (page 169) to this dish.

- 1 tbsp EVOO
- ½ lb. shiitakes
- 1½ cups kale (deveined and chopped)
- ½ cup diced red onion
- 6 oz. goat cheese (crumbled)
- 6 oz. Manchego or goat Gouda (grated)
- optional: Ranchero Pinto Beans (page 169)
- optional: 2 chipotles in adobo

1. Preheat the oven to 375 °F.

2. Heat the oil over medium heat in a large skillet.

3. Add the mushrooms, kale, and onion and cook, stirring frequently, for about 10 minutes.

4. In a medium-sized bowl add kale along with the cheeses and optional beans and chipotles. Toss until combined.

5. Oil a casserole dish and add in the cheese & kale mix. Bake until bubbling for about 25 minutes. Serve hot.

Chinese Snow Pea and Broccoli Stir Fry (V)

Snow peas are packed with vitamin A, iron, potassium, dietary fiber, magnesium, and folic acid. They are also a good source of vitamin C which neutralizes free radicals, and reduces oxidative stress. The potassium and vitamin C help to protect your heart and reduce blood pressure.

Ginger is anti-inflammatory, aids digestion, and can help reduce arthritic pain. Ginger can also reduce your risk of diabetes and may help fight cancer. And for my workout fanatics there is good news, ginger has been shown to reduce exercise related muscle soreness.

- Teriyaki Dipping Sauce (page 139)
- 3 tbsp avocado oil
- 2 cups broccoli florets
- 1 cup fennel
- 2 cups carrot (spiralized)
- ¼ cup rice cooking wine
- 2 cups snow peas
- 2 scallions (chopped)
- 4 shiitakes chopped
- Grain of choice

1. Prepare the Teriyaki Dipping Sauce (page 139) and set aside.

2. Pour the avocado oil into a large skillet or wok. Add the broccoli, fennel, and carrots and sauté for 3-4 minutes.

3. Add rice cooking wine and stir. Add the sauce, snow peas, scallions and shiitake. Sauté for another 5-6 minutes. Add grains and stir for one minute. Serve immediately.

Coconut Flour Wraps/Burritos (DF)

I love paleo wraps, but the additives and extras can be a big "oh no!" for reducing inflammation. You can keep this simple or add some awesome spices to jazz this up, from curry to tarragon to berbere spice, the options are endless.

Coconut flour is completely gluten-free and very versatile. It can replicate wheat-based recipes like pancakes and flatbreads. It's a pretty good source of protein too, 2 tbsp has 5 grams of protein!

Have you ever wondered how coconut flour is made and where it comes from? It's made from coconut pulp. To make coconut milk, you must soak the coconut meat. That coconut meat that is left over is then dried out and ground into a flour.

If you are frying foods, you can try using coconut flour instead of regular flour or almond flour to make your recipes gluten and nut free. It cannot be a substitute fpr either of these flours in baking recipes however. It will always require much more egg to rise than other flours.

- 4 eggs
- ¼ cup coconut flour
- 2 tbsp flax seeds
- ¼ cup coconut milk or rice milk
- EVOO for sautéing (medium heat)

1. Add the eggs, coconut flour, flax, and milk to a medium mixing bowl, whisking thoroughly.
2. Let sit for 5 minutes to thicken.
3. Add 1-2 tbsp of EVOO to a medium-sized skillet and use 2 tbsp of batter for each wrap. Cook until browned for 1-2 minutes, then flip and cook on the other side.
4. Makes 6 mini wraps. Fill with vegetables and proteins of your choice!

Ethiopian Collards (V)

You can get berbere from one of my favorite spice stores, Penzey's[3]. I know this dish was the real deal when I had a bunch of Ethiopian friends over for dinner, and they asked where I got this recipe from! Penzey's rocks for amazing salt-free blends.

Collards are a good vegan source of calcium. It is also rich in iron and fiber and is a moderate source of protein. One cup of collards provides 8 grams of fiber and is incredibly rich in vitamin K which improves calcium absorption. Collard greens also contain alpha-lipoic acid which can lower glucose levels, increase insulin sensitivity, and reduce the effects of oxidative stress. High levels of oxidative stress can lead to diabetes, cancer, premature aging, Parkinson's, Alzheimer's and heart disease.

- 2 bunches collard greens (1½-1¾ lb.; stemmed and finely chopped)
- 2 tbsp EVOO
- 1 cup minced red onion
- 2 tbsp minced fresh garlic
- 1 tbsp berbere
- ¼ cup low-reactive tomato sauce (page 131)
- ¾ tsp sea salt
- Grains of choice

1. Bring a large pot of water to a boil over high heat. Add the collards and cook until soft for about 15 minutes.

2. Drain well in a colander. Add the EVOO and onion to the pot and cook 4-5 minutes over medium heat, stirring often, until the onion is translucent.

3. Add the garlic and berbere and cook for one minute until fragrant.

4. Add collards back in with tomato sauce and sea salt.

5. Turn heat to simmer and cook for 5-6 minutes.

6. Serve warm with grains of choice.

---

[3] www.penzeys.com

Fennel al Forno

Fennel is of the first vegetables I have someone test right after potato (as long as it's cooked; raw fennel is a MESS for most people's digestion). Cooking fennel bulbs makes the anise flavor so mild, and the texture is so much like cooked celery: delicious, warming, and so soothing on your stomach.

With the cheese and almonds this is a perfect lunch protein. For dinner you would need to add another protein. This dish is super low starch, so you could do beans, grains, or potatoes and be a happy camper.

You could keep it *super* low starch by adding in something like the Broccoli with Sunflower Tahini (see page 137) for a perfect dinner meal.

- 4 medium fennel bulbs (with a few green fronds reserved)
- Sea salt and pepper
- ¼ cup EVOO (plus more to oil the baking dish)
- ½ tsp celery seed (optional)
- 3 garlic cloves (finely chopped)
- 1 tsp chopped rosemary
- ¼ cup coarse, dry, homemade bread crumbs or almond flour
- 1 cup grated Manchego
- ½ cup almonds slivers
- 2 tbsp fennel fronds

1. Heat oven to 375 °F. Remove the top layer of the fennel bulbs. Cut the fennel crosswise into half-inch-thick slices. Bring a large pot of water to a boil. Boil the fennel for 1 minute, then put it in a bowl of cold water, drain, and pat dry. Season it with sea salt and pepper. Oil an oven-proof baking dish and add the fennel.

2. In a small bowl, stir together 3 tablespoons of EVOO, celery seed, garlic, and chopped rosemary. Drizzle 2 tablespoons of this mixture over the fennel. Add the breadcrumbs and drizzle the remaining oil over it. Top with grated Manchego cheese.

3. Bake for 20-25 minutes until nicely browned. Remove from oven and add almond slivers return to oven and broil on high for 2 minutes. Remove from oven and garnish with the chopped fennel fronds. Serve warm.

"Fried" Chickpeas (V)

Chickpeas are rich in iron, phosphorus, magnesium, copper, and zinc minerals, Chickpeas are among the richest sources of vitamin B6, which makes the neurotransmitters serotonin (your "I'm happy hormone") and norepinephrine (stress coping). Vitamin B6 also helps the body make melatonin, a hormone that aids deep sleep. Chickpeas are also rich in B5, which aids a healthy digestive tract and normal hormone production.

Whole Foods has a no-salt canned chickpea and Goya has a low-sodium version. If you can't find those, try to pick a brand that has less than 150 mg of sodium per ounce.

I use avocado oil for baking when temperatures exceed 375 °F.

- 2 (15 oz.) cans low-sodium chickpeas (drained and rinsed)
- 3 tbsp avocado oil
- 1 tsp cumin
- ½ tsp coriander
- ½ tsp cayenne
- Salt and pepper to taste

1. Preheat the oven to 425 °F.
2. Spread the chickpeas on a towel and dry completely.
3. In a bowl mix all ingredients.
4. Add the chickpea mix to a baking sheet.
5. Roast for 20 minutes, stir the chickpeas, then roast for another 20 minutes or until the chickpeas are brown and crisp.
6. Remove from the oven and serve warm. Save any leftovers for snacking later!

Greek Twice-Baked Potatoes (V)

Olives are a great source of vitamin E, which neutralizes free radicals and reduces heart attack and cancer risk. Hydroxytyrosol, an olive phytonutrient, is also a cancer fighter and may also help prevent bone loss. As vegan diets can be lower in calcium, this is an important fruit to include. Olive extract is histamine-reducing, so it can fight allergies and aid weight loss. Due to olives higher sodium content, best to limit to 3-4 per serving.

Both the pesto and nutritional yeast will boost protein. The nutritional yeast has the added benefit of imparting a cheese like taste.

- 1½ pound small red potatoes
- 4 tbsp EVOO
- ½ tsp sea salt
- ¼ tsp black pepper
- ½ tsp garlic powder
- ½ tsp oregano
- ½ tsp thyme

- ½ tsp onion powder
- ½ cup coconut milk
- ½ cup cooked broccoli (chopped)
- ¼ cup Kalamata olives (chopped)
- ½ cup pesto of choice or nutritional yeast (optional)

1. Preheat the oven to 375 °F. Oil a baking sheet with 2 tbsp of EVOO.

2. Wash the potatoes and pat them dry with a towel. Put the potatoes in large bowl and toss with EVOO, sea salt, herbs and spices, making sure that all the potatoes are covered with a thin layer of oil.

3. Place the potatoes onto a baking sheet. Bake for approximately 30 minutes or until soft or fork tender. Remove from oven and allow to cool.

4. Once cooled, cut the top off the potatoes, and using a spoon or melon baller, scoop out the potato, leaving the skin and a thin layer of potato inside. Place the scooped-out potato into a medium-sized bowl. Place the potato skins back onto the baking sheet.

5. Mash up the potato in the bowl and pour in the coconut milk and continue mashing. Add the broccoli, and olives.

6. Spoon the potato mixture back into the potato skins.

7. Place the baking tray back into the oven and cook for an additional 10 minutes until the top of the potatoes are slightly crispy. Optional topping with pesto or nutritional yeast.

Grilled Radicchio with Apple and Orange Peel (V)

If you don't want to grill the radicchio, you can opt to sauté or broil it. Organic orange peel is a great cancer fighter. All bitter vegetables are great for gall bladder function, which supports liver health.

Garlic can lower blood pressure and reduce oxidative stress. This combo of health benefits may reduce the risk of common cognitive disorders like dementia. The sulfur compounds in garlic can help reduce heavy metals in your body. It is also a powerful immune booster and can shorten the duration of a cold. Compounds found in garlic have been identified as effective in destroying the cells in glioblastomas, a type of deadly brain tumor that John McCain passed from in 2018.

Another compound in garlic, was 100 times more effective than two popular antibiotics in fighting bacteria that causes intestinal infections.

Dressing

- ⅓ cup EVOO
- ¼ cup balsamic vinegar
- 6 garlic cloves (chopped)
- 1 tbsp fresh rosemary (chopped)
- 1 tsp finely grated organic orange peel

- 4 large heads of radicchio (each quartered through core end)
- sea salt and pepper
- 1 apple (chopped)
- ½ cup pecan pesto (page 134) or sunflower tahini (page 137)

1. Whisk the oil, vinegar, garlic, rosemary, and orange peel in a large bowl. Add the radicchio and toss to coat. Marinate for 15 minutes.

2. Prepare the barbecue (medium heat). Drain the marinade into a small bowl. Place the radicchio on the grill and sprinkle with salt and pepper. Grill the radicchio until the edges are crisp and slightly charred, turning occasionally (about 6 minutes). Transfer the radicchio to a serving platter, top with chopped apple, and drizzle with reserved marinade and pesto or tahini.

Guacamole Onion Rings (DF)

If onions are healthy, and avocados are healthy, then guacamole onion rings must be super-duper healthy!! Well, yes, they can be! Get ready to make this a regular on your menu. Like most of my recipes, it's easy to make this one gluten-free.

Avocado oil may reduce the pain and stiffness of arthritis. It high in oleic acid, so it's a cancer fighter. It is also rich monounsaturated fats and vitamins A, E and D to boost immune function, skin and bone health, hormonal balance, and thyroid function.

- 3 ripe avocados
- 1 lime
- 1 tomato (diced)
- 2 cloves garlic (minced)
- ¼ tsp sea salt
- ½ tsp cumin
- ¼ tsp cayenne
- ¼ tsp cinnamon
- 2 medium yellow onions
- 2 eggs
- 2 cups panko (or gluten-free panko)
- Avocado oil for frying
- 2 limes cut into wedges

1. Using a medium-sized mixing bowl, mash the avocados with the juice of one lime. Mix in the chopped tomato and spices.

2. Cut the onion into ½-inch slices. Place wax paper on a baking tray, separate the onion rounds, and fill with approximately one teaspoon of guacamole. Place the tray in a freezer for an hour.

3. Beat eggs in one bowl and put the panko in separate bowl. Remove the frozen onions from the freezer. Gently dredge the onion in the egg and then in the panko. Repeat this step for extra crispy onion rings.

4. Using a large skillet, fill the base with avocado oil, ¼-inch thick, on medium-high heat. Fry the onion rings until browned and then flip and fry on other side. Place on a plate with towels to drain the excess oil. Repeat until done. Serve with lime wedges.

Hemp Seed Hummus (V)

Hemp is such a great vegan protein source and is rich in so many nutrients that are essential for thyroid function such as zinc, iron, magnesium, calcium, potassium, and omega 3. It is slightly higher in omega 6 (the pro-inflammatory omega), but because vegetarian and vegan diets are lower in omega 6, you would not have to be as concerned with this as in an omnivore diet. Hemp seeds may reduce symptoms related to PMS and menopause, thanks to its high levels of gamma-linolenic acid (GLA).

- 1 head garlic
- 1 medium to large zucchini (chopped)
- ⅓ cup hemp seeds
- 2 tbsp sunflower seeds
- 2 tbsp lemon juice
- 2 tbsp EVOO (divided)
- 1 tbsp dried rosemary
- ⅛ tsp sea salt
- ¼ tsp grated organic lemon or organic orange zest (optional)

1. Preheat the oven to 300 °F. Slice off the top of garlic head and drizzle with EVOO. Place the garlic in a small roasting dish, roasting for 40 minutes or until cloves are soft to the touch.

2. Allow the garlic to cool. Squeeze the roasted garlic cloves out of their skins with your hands or pull out with a small cocktail fork.

3. Combine the roasted garlic, zucchini, hemp seeds, sunflower seeds, lemon juice, EVOO, rosemary, and salt in a food processor and blend for 1 minute. Transfer to a serving bowl and top with zest, if desired.

Jalapeno Poppers

Looking for Sunday football recipes? How about healthy jalapeno poppers? You can use this with any of my sauces as a dip.

Studies have suggested that jalapeno peppers may provide pain relief for migraine headaches, and like all chilis, jalapenos can boost metabolism and lower inflammation.

This recipe has the option to be gluten-free and egg free. If you want crispier poppers you can substitute egg for the coconut milk.

- 15 jalapenos (see note)
- 8 oz. chèvre goat cheese
- 6 oz. grated goat Gouda
- ½ cup flour or rice flour
- 1 tsp garlic powder
- 1 tsp onion powder
- ½ cup coconut milk or unflavored rice milk (or eggs)
- ½ cup panko or gluten-free panko
- 2 cups avocado oil
- Sauce of choice

1. Slice the jalapenos in half lengthwise. If you want mild poppers, use a spoon to remove the pith and seeds. If you want some fire, only remove half. Using a small mixing bowl, combine the goat cheese and then spoon the mixture into each jalapeno. Set aside.

2. Add the flour, garlic, and onion powder in a small mixing bowl. Mix well. Dip each jalapeno into the seasoned flour mixture, and let the peppers dry for 10 minutes (If you omit this step, the coating will just fall off!).

3. Arrange the coconut milk and panko into two separate bowls. Dip the jalapeno into the coconut milk, then immediately into the panko, and place on a rack. For extra crispy poppers, dip the jalapenos a second time!

4. Place the oil in a medium skillet over medium-high heat, and fry the poppers, 4-5 at a time, 2 minutes on each side. Let the poppers drain on a paper towel on a plate. Serve with sauce of choice.

Note: You may want to wear kitchen gloves when handling jalapenos.

Lavash – Armenian Flatbread (DF)

While many people think that they have an issue with gluten or wheat, the real culprit may be the yeast or baking powder. For folks who want a clean wheat bread recipe, I would suggest starting with lavash. Black pepper aids weight loss, improves digestion, relieves colds and coughs, and boosts metabolism.

00 flour is a light fine flour that many people find easier to digest. You can buy 00 flour produced in North America, but many people feel that the flour from Italy is best.

It is theorized that it is not the hybridization that makes wheat so much tougher to digest in the US, but the controversial use of the herbicide Roundup which contains the toxic ingredient glyphosate. It is sprayed on wheat several days before harvest to increase the yield of the crops.

You can buy 00 flour in Italian specialty stores and online.

This recipe is amazing for making grilled pizzas, wraps or burritos.

- 2½ cups all-purpose flour, spelt or 00 flour
- 1 tsp sugar
- 1 tsp sea salt
- ⅔ cup water
- 1 egg white
- 2 tbsp avocado oil
- 2 tsp coarsely ground black pepper

1. Preheat the oven to 400 °F.

2. Stir the flour, sugar, and salt in a large bowl. Add the water, egg white, and avocado oil; mix well. Knead until the dough is smooth (approx. 5 minutes). You can also mix in a food processor.

3. Divide the dough into 10 balls. Roll each ball on a lightly floured surface until paper thin, almost translucent. Place the dough on a lightly greased baking pan and sprinkle with pepper. Bake until golden brown and crisp, about 12–15 minutes, and serve with toppings of choice.

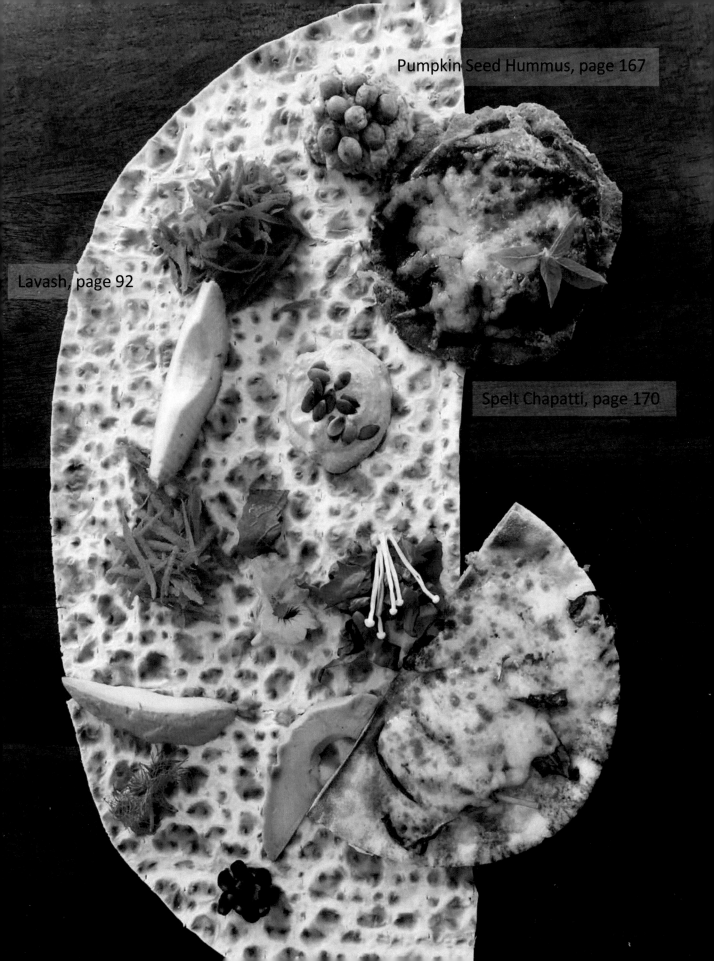

Pumpkin Seed Hummus, page 167

Lavash, page 92

Spelt Chapatti, page 170

Lemon Garlic Hummus (V)

This dish is a great way to sneak in any vegetable for picky kids. I alternate vegetables like kale, spinach, or broccoli to make this protein rich, but it's also great to add in neutral vegetables such as zucchini and yellow squash. Caramelized onions work well too! If you have any leftover roasted or cooked vegetables, then add them to this dish. They are amazing and add quite a bit of depth to your hummus.

Roasting garlic tones down the strong garlic flavor and makes for a milder, sweeter and creamier taste. I love baking several heads at a time to add to stews, casseroles and sauces.

You can add the hemp seeds to boost protein.

- 1 head garlic
- EVOO for drizzling
- 2 cans low-sodium chickpeas
- 2 cups cooked kale

- ½ cup hemp seeds (optional)
- ½ cup sunflower tahini
- ½ cup lemon juice
- Sea salt and pepper to taste

1. Preheat the oven to 300 °F. Slice off the garlic head and drizzle with EVOO. Place the garlic in a roasting dish and roast for 40 minutes until the cloves are soft to the touch.

2. Allow the garlic to cool. Squeeze the roasted garlic cloves out of their skins with your hands or pull out with a small cocktail fork.

3. Add all the ingredients to a food processor and blend.

Panko Broccoli Delicata Gratin

Casserole dishes are my fave to make in winter, it warms up the house and makes several meals for the week, if you double this recipe.

Delicata squash is a great low carb vegetable. It has only 8 grams of carbs per cup, roughly half the level of butternut or pumpkin squash.

A cup of delicata has your total daily requirements for vitamin A to support your vision and healthy skin. It is also a good source of vitamin C for immune function and collagen growth.

- 2 lb. broccoli florets
- 1 large delicata squash (chopped into 1-inch cubes)
- 1 large red onion (chopped)
- 2 tbsp EVOO

- 2 tbsp unsalted butter (melted)
- 2 garlic cloves (minced)
- ⅓ cup panko
- 1 cup grated Manchego

1. Adjust an oven rack to the upper-middle position and another to the middle position. Preheat the oven to 400 °F.

2. Add the broccoli, delicata, red onion and EVOO to a bowl and toss.

3. Add vegetables to a casserole dish and roast for 30 minutes

4. In a bowl add butter, garlic, panko and manchego. Mix well.

5. Remove the sheet pan from the oven and sprinkle the broccoli with the panko cheese mix. Turn the broiler to high. Broil until the cheese is melted and browned, or for about 2 minutes. Remove from the oven and serve warm.

Panko Crusted Brussels Sprouts with Pecan Pesto (V)

Brussels sprouts are a goitrogen, so limit their use for your thyroid health and metabolism. The key to making them easier to digest is to steam them well first, then sauté or roast! Brussels are very high in iron and vitamin A. and also rich in vitamin K which promotes healthy bones. Brussels contain kaempferol which neutralizes free radicals, improves heart health and may slow cancer cell growth.

- 1 cup pecan pesto (page 134)
- 2 lb. Brussels sprouts (trimmed and halved & steamed for 5 minutes)
- Avocado oil (for roasting)
- 2 garlic cloves (minced)
- 2 tbsp EVOO
- 1 cup panko
- Lemon wedges and chopped tarragon (for garnish)

1. Prepare pecan pesto (page 134) and set aside.
2. Preheat the oven to 375 °F.
3. Steam the halved Brussels sprouts in a pot for 5 minutes.
4. Place the Brussels sprouts in an oiled baking dish.
5. Sauté the garlic in EVOO in a skillet, add the panko, and mix.
6. Sprinkle the panko mix on the Brussel sprouts and bake for 20 minutes.
7. Remove the sprouts from the oven and drizzle with pecan pesto.
8. Top the Brussels sprouts with tarragon and serve with lemon wedges.

Panko Crusted Brussels Sprouts with Pecan Pesto, page 96

Persian Dill Rice and Peas

Dill can reduce histamine to fight allergies and is also a decongestant. Dill is good to have when you are fighting a cold, as it can prevent common respiratory disorders. Its histamine-reducing properties also make it a valuable herb to include if you have asthma or migraines.

A recent study found that individuals who consumed higher quantities of almonds, walnuts, and peanuts had their risk of breast cancer reduced by 2-3 times.

Basmati originates from India, and it contains nearly 20% more fiber than most brown rices. Fiber can protect against many forms of cancer, but colon cancer is at the top of the list. Basmati rice contains B1, which is commonly referred to as a "brain vitamin." In one study, B1 was noted as a positive nutrient in treating patients with Alzheimer's. The higher starch of this makes it perfect for a longer workout day.

- 2 cups white basmati rice (soaked in cold water for 1 hour, then drained)
- 4 cups water or vegetable stock
- 4 tbsp butter
- 2 cups peas
- 1 bunch fresh dill (roughly chopped)
- ½ tsp saffron (soaked in 1 tbsp hot water)
- Sea salt & pepper to taste
- ½ cup almond slivers or walnuts
- Garnish of mint, basil, or cilantro

1. Using a medium-sized pot, bring the rice and water to a boil. Reduce the heat to low, cover, and simmer for 22–25 minutes, or until the rice has absorbed all the water. Add 2 tbsp of butter, mix, and set aside.

2. Using a large skillet, heat the remaining 2 tbsp of butter over medium-low heat. Add the peas and dill and sauté, stirring occasionally until the dill is wilted. Remove from heat.

3. In a large bowl, combine the cooked rice, peas, and saffron until thoroughly mixed. Season to taste with salt and pepper and top with almonds and herbs of choice.

Persian Saffron Rice with Barberries (V)

Persians are famous for their rice and for a very good reason. The inimitable flavor of saffron delicately scents this dish, and the mix of lime and cranberries are divine. Almonds add crunch and protein, but you could use any nut for this dish. I am partial to pecans or walnuts.

Saffron has traditionally been in used in Iran for insomnia, heartburn, depression, gas, PMS, and cramps.

You can buy rose water syrup and barberries at Middle Eastern markets. Barberries are a powerful liver and gall bladder detoxifier. It is antimicrobial and can help fight infection.

Rose water is used to ease depression, soothe sore throats, is good for digestion, fights infection, is anti-inflammatory, and is reputed to be an aphrodisiac!

- 1 cup white basmati rice (soaked in cold water for 1 hour, then drained)
- 2 cups water
- 2 tbsp butter
- ½ tsp sea salt
- Pinch of turmeric
- ¼ cup slivered almonds
- 1 tbsp EVOO
- ½ cup dried barberries soaked in 1/4 cup hot water
- 1 tbsp agave or honey
- ½ tsp saffron (soaked in 1 tbsp hot water)
- ½ teaspoon rose water syrup
- ½ teaspoon organic orange zest
- dried rose petals (optional)
- almond slivers for garnish

1. Using a medium-sized pot, bring the rice and water to a boil. Reduce the heat to low, cover, and simmer for 22–25 minutes, or until the rice has absorbed all the water. Add 2 tbsp of butter, mix, and set aside.

2. Add the almonds to a dry skillet on medium heat and toast for 30 seconds. Remove and set aside. Add 1 tbsp EVOO and reduce the heat to low. Drain the barberries and add them to the skillet. Sauté for one minute, then add agave. Add the saffron and the rose water. Stir well.

3. Add rice to a bowl or platter. Mix all ingredients together. When serving garnish with orange zest and optional rose petals and almond slivers.

Potato and Leek Gratin

Leeks are a close cousin to garlic and onions yet have a much milder flavor. Leeks are rich in allicin, which helps reduce cholesterol. They are also antibacterial, antifungal, and antiviral. Leeks are very high in inulin which is a type of fiber that is not digested in the small intestine. Instead it travels to the lower gut and acts as a prebiotic to feed friendly bacteria and can work to promote better digestive health. Inulin is also linked to better weight loss and better blood sugar. It is being studied for its positive effects on non-alcoholic fatty liver disease.

Marjoram is a member of the mint and oregano family. It is similar to oregano but slightly sweeter, more delicate and not as spicy. Marjoram improves your digestion by increasing production of digestive enzymes. It can help alleviate common digestive disorders such as gas, abdominal cramping, and constipation. Marjoram contains compounds that are antibacterial, antiviral and antifungal, helping you fight runny noses, cough, colds and flu, food poisoning and infections.

- 2 tbsp unsalted butter (or avocado oil)
- 2 large leeks (trimmed and halved lengthwise)
- 1½ lb. Yukon gold potatoes
- 1 tsp marjoram
- ½ tsp dried sage
- 1 cup coconut cream
- 1 fat garlic clove (finely chopped)
- 1 bay leaf
- ½ tsp nutmeg
- ¾ cup goat Gouda (grated)

1. Heat the oven to 350 °F and oil a casserole dish.

2. Wash the leeks to remove any grit and slice thinly crosswise. Slice the potatoes into rounds, ¹/₈-inch thick.

3. Layer the potato in the casserole dish.

4. Melt the 2 tbsp of butter in a large skillet over medium heat. Add the leeks, marjoram and sage.

5. Cook, stirring, until the leeks are tender and golden (about 5–7 minutes).

6. Add the coconut cream, garlic, and bay leaf to the skillet. Simmer for 5 minutes and stir in the nutmeg. Remove the bay leaf.

7. Pour the leeks over the potatoes, and top with the Gouda. Transfer to the oven. Bake for 40–50 minutes, or until the cheese is bubbling and golden. Serve warm.

Roasted Broccoli with Tahini Sauce and Pomegranate (V)

This is another crowd-pleasing dish that is easy to prepare. Broccoli helps lower cancer risk, promotes bone health, and aids detoxification.

Pomegranate has numerous health benefits, ranging from fighting cancer to reducing arthritic symptoms. It aids digestion for people with Crohn's, ulcerative colitis, and IBS and may help fight Alzheimer's.

- 1 cup sunflower tahini (page 137)
- 1 to 1½ lb. broccoli (chopped)
- 2 tbsp EVOO
- Sea salt and freshly ground pepper to taste
- ½ cup pomegranate arils
- ½ tsp organic orange zest
- 2 cups cooked wild rice for serving or grains of choice

1. Prepare sunflower tahini (page 136) and set aside. Preheat oven to 450 °F.

2. Oil a baking sheet. In a bowl add the broccoli and mix with EVOO and add sea salt and pepper. Place the broccoli on the baking sheet in an even layer. Roast until the tops are nicely browned, about 35 minutes in total.

3. Remove from the oven and transfer onto a platter or to individual serving plates. Drizzle on the tahini sauce and top with pomegranate and orange zest. Serve with wild rice or grains of choice.

Beet Ceviche, page 46

Wild Rice, Almond, and Cranberry Dressing, page 113

Roasted Broccoli with Tahini Sauce and Pomegranate, page 101

Roasted Fennel and Yellow Squash with Manchego

Yellow squash is a nutrient-dense vegetable for sure. It's loaded with vitamins A, B2, B6, and C. It's also rich in folate, magnesium, fiber, and potassium. These nutrients are invaluable for fighting cancer and heart disease. Yellow squash is also rich in manganese which helps boost bone strength.

Adults should be consuming 4-5,000 mg of potassium a day yet less than 2% do. Potassium decreases the risk of stroke, protects muscle mass, preserves bone density, and reduces the formation of kidney stones. It helps to control the electrical activity of the heart and all of your muscles.

This dish has roughly 2500 mg of potassium, if you were to add two cup of beans that would bring it to 4,000 mg!

- 3-4 fennel bulbs (reserve fronds for garnish)
- 2 large yellow squashes (chopped)
- Fresh ground black pepper
- 1 tsp sage
- ⅓ cup freshly grated Manchego
- Serve with hummus, beans or grains of choice

1. Preheat the oven to 350 °F.
2. Trim off and discard the bottom and tough outer layer of each fennel bulb. Cut each bulb in half from top to bottom, then cut each half into 2 equal wedges, keeping the core intact; this will help hold the wedges together.
3. Place fennel and zucchini in a large oiled baking dish.
4. Sprinkle with pepper and sage and then top with cheese. Bake for 30 minutes until cheese is browned.
5. Garnish with the fronds and serve warm with hummus, beans or grains of choice.

Sage Potato Gratin

Sage is one of my FAVORITE herbs, it's great for hot flashes and so much more! Research has shown that even small amounts of sage can increase short term and long-term memory (even with Alzheimer's). It's great for respiratory and GI issues as well as for gout and arthritis. It is also antimicrobial, antibacterial, and anti-inflammatory.

This dish is already a protein rich lunch thanks to the potato, pumpkin seeds and cheese, but if you are working out and need more protein this would be amazing with kale.

- 1 can coconut milk
- ½ tsp sea salt
- 4-5 fresh sage leaves (finely chopped)
- 2 lb. red potatoes
- 1 cup pumpkin seeds
- Cayenne pepper or chipotle powder for a smoky taste
- 1 cup grated Manchego cheese

1. Preheat the oven to 375 °F.

2. Oil an 8 x 8-inch casserole dish.

3. Using a medium pot, add the coconut milk, salt, and the sage leaves.

4. Bring to a simmer for 5-6 minutes. While simmering, slice the potatoes $1/8$-inch thick.

5. Begin to layer the potatoes on the bottom of the dish. After completing the first layer, season with cayenne pepper or chipotle, and sprinkle with cheese and pumpkin seeds.

6. Pour the cream over the casserole. Sprinkle the remaining cheese evenly over the top of the potatoes.

7. Place the dish in the oven and bake for 40–45 minutes until the potatoes are tender and the cheese is browned. Serve immediately.

Spicy Roasted Sunflower Seeds (V)

Can you use any nut or seed for this recipe? Of course! I'm just especially fond of sunflower seeds because they are such a great source of selenium, which nourishes your thyroid and metabolism.

The benefits of selenium include its ability to increase immunity and help the body fight free radicals and inflammation. It can also boost cognitive function and is an essential nutrient for fertility for men and women. It supports cardiovascular health and can help asthma. It plays a role in the maintenance of glutathione, which is important for liver health as well preventing damage from free radicals, peroxides, lipid peroxides, and heavy metals.

Sunflower seeds are an excellent source of vitamin E which is important for skin health and maintenance. It helps to protect your skin from UV ray damage.

- 2 cups sunflower seeds
- 2 tbsp EVOO, plus more for baking sheet
- ½ tsp chipotle or cayenne
- ½ tsp cumin
- ½ tsp garlic powder
- ½ tsp onion powder
- ¼ tsp salt

1. Preheat your oven to 250 degrees °F.
2. Oil the baking sheet.
3. Add the sunflower seeds, EVOO, and spices to the bowl and mix thoroughly. Add more oil if needed.
4. Pour the sunflower seeds on the baking sheet and spread evenly.
5. Bake in the oven for about 20-25 minutes or until golden. Let it cool first before serving.

Stuffed Figs with Goat Cheese, Nuts, Thyme, and Honey

Try this incredibly elegant recipe as an easy hors d'oeuvres for your dinner parties.

Figs are high in fiber and a good source of vitamins A, B1 and B2, as well as iron, magnesium, calcium, and potassium.

Almonds support heart health, with nutrients like magnesium, copper, manganese, calcium, and potassium. Studies have shown they can lower the "bad" cholesterol (LDL), especially in individuals with diabetes.

Hazelnuts lower inflammation and can boost brain function and help to manage diabetes.

Refined salt is heavily processed and involves bleaching and iodizing. Sea salt involves very little processing, so it retains its minerals (over 80!).

- 12 medium-sized fresh figs
- 4 oz. soft goat cheese
- 4 tbsp chopped almonds or hazelnuts
- 1 tbsp chopped thyme
- 2 tbsp Manukah honey
- Sea salt
- Toasted bread or salad

1. Preheat the oven to 375 °F.
2. Cut off the stems and make an X cut at the top of each fig, half way through.
3. Stuff the figs with soft goat cheese using a small spoon.
4. Sprinkle some chopped nuts and thyme over your stuffed figs and drizzle them with honey.
5. Bake for about 5 minutes or until they look soft and start to release juice. Then broil for one minute until cheese is browned.
6. Add a sprinkle of sea salt to the figs.
7. Serve on toasted bread or salad.

Stuffed Zucchini Blossoms (V)

When I look at most recipes for squash blossoms, I am immediately daunted. TOO many steps! I don't have the time to boil, ice water bath, and woo squash blossoms with an interpretive dance of my love, do you? Here are 2 easy-to-make versions: one vegan, one vegetarian.

Stuffed Blossoms (Vegan version):

- 8–10 zucchini blossoms
- 1 cup hummus
- ½ cup panko

1. Stuff each zucchini blossom with 1 tbsp of hummus.
2. Roll the squash blossoms in the hummus (approx. 2 tsp per blossom) and dredge through the panko; set aside.
3. When all the blossoms have been prepared, follow the cooking directions below.

Stuffed Blossoms (Vegetarian version):

- 8–10 zucchini blossoms
- ½ cup goat cheese
- ½ cup mango cucumber salsa (page 133) or salsa of choice
- ½ cup panko

1. Combine the goat cheese and salsa (equal ratio), and stuff the blossoms with 1 tbsp of goat cheese/salsa mix.
2. Roll the blossoms in the goat cheese mix and then dredge through the panko.
3. When all the blossoms have been prepared, follow the cooking directions below.

Cooking directions:

1. Preheat the oven to 375 °F. Place blossoms in a lightly oiled medium cast-iron skillet and then place 2 cups of panko in the skillet. Lay blossoms on top (the panko keeps them from getting burned) and bake at 375 °F for 10 minutes.
2. Serve warm.

Sugar Snap Peas with Mint and Orange (V)

Here is a great recipe to test snap peas, or you could use snow peas, which are even less reactive.

Make sure to get organic oranges, as pesticides lurk in the oil of the rind. Pesticides are endocrine disruptors which create hormonal imbalance and are linked to diseases like cancer.

Snap peas are high in vitamin C, which speeds wound healing, boosts immune function, and aids in the production of collagen.

Peas are a good source of folate for heart health and help to maintain a healthy pregnancy. They are also a good source of iron to boost your energy levels and help to fight anemia. Peas are very high in fiber which means great digestion, adding a grain or soup to this would increase fiber even more and keep you full all day.

- 3 cups snap peas (trimmed)
- 2 tbsp butter
- 2 tbsp thinly sliced fresh mint leaves
- ½ tsp finely grated organic orange peel
- Sea salt and pepper
- Serve with grains, salad or soup of choice

1. Using a large saucepan, cook the peas in boiling water for 3-4 minutes; drain and let stand at room temperature.
2. Melt the butter in a medium-sized skillet over medium-high heat.
3. Stir in the mint and orange peel; add the sugar snap peas; and sauté just until it is heated through (about 1 minute).
4. Season with sea salt and pepper. Transfer to a bowl and serve with grains, salad or soup of choice.

Thanksgiving Stuffed Delicata (V)

Delicata is such an easy, elegant vegetable to stuff and serve at holidays or special occasions. The slight sweetness of delicata pairs well with tart fruits like cranberries or raspberries. Because it's lower in starch than most winter vegetables, you can add more vegetables that are higher in carbs like potatoes, or grains like wheat.

The variations on this squash are literally endless. It's also a great vehicle for repurposing leftover vegetables. To do this just bake the delicata for 30 minutes, then stuff with leftovers, add bake to the oven and bake for 10 minutes more.

Vegetarian

- 1 fennel (chopped fine)
- 2 delicatas
- 2 cups kale, deveined and chopped fine
- ½ cup cooked wild rice
- 6 oz grated manchego

Vegan

- 2 delicatas
- 1 fennel (chopped fine)
- 2 cups cooked kale, deveined and chopped fine
- 1 cup pumpkin pesto
- ½ cup cooked wild rice
- EVOO for baking pan

1. Preheat oven to 375 °F.

1. In a small pot add 1/2 cup water, bring to boil and steam fennel for 5 minutes,

2. Cut ends on delicatas. Cut in half then scoop out seeds and discard or save for baking (seeds are delicious baked with cinnamon and cayenne). You can cut the delicata in half again to make 4 pieces.

3. Remove fennel from pot and place fennel in a colander to drain dry.

4. Stuff the delicata, layering all ingredients in order.

5. Oil a baking sheet with EVOO and place the delicata manchego side up for vegetarian and wild rice side up for vegan.

6. Bake for 40 minutes until delicata is tender to the touch. Serve with your holiday main dish.

The Cleanse Oven-Roasted Vegetables, page 111

The Cleanse **Oven-Roasted Vegetables** (V)

Once *The Cleanse* is over, you can add other vegetables to this base recipe. It's especially good with fennel, potatoes and winter squash like delicata and butternut. Roasting does intensify the sugars, so limit to a couple of times a week.

To boost protein, you could easily add cheese or a pesto or grains to this.

Leftover vegetables will add complexity to your soups, hummus or croquettes.

- 2 zucchinis (chopped)
- 2 yellow squash (chopped)
- 1 red onion (chopped)
- 4 carrots (chopped)
- 2 heads of broccoli (chopped)
- 4 garlic cloves (chopped)
- ¼ cup EVOO
- 1 tbsp Herbes de Provence (page 127)

1. Preheat the oven to 375 °F.
2. Using a large bowl, mix all the ingredients; spread on a baking sheet; and bake for 45 minutes or until the vegetables are tender. Serve warm.

Teriyaki Escarole and Scallion Pancakes (DF)

This is a pretty fun recipe because you could make it a savory breakfast, a quick lunch, or a nice light easy dinner with a side salad and some roasted vegetables. Escarole is rich in nutrients, such as selenium and zinc, which support thyroid health. It's also a good source of B vitamins.

- 4 eggs
- 1 cup all-purpose flour
- ¼ cup chopped scallions
- 1 cup chopped escarole
- 1 tsp coconut aminos
- ½ tsp sesame oil
- ½ tsp cumin
- ½ tsp garlic powder
- ½ tsp onion powder
- ½ tsp sea salt
- Dash cayenne
- 2-3 tbsp avocado oil

Dipping Sauce:

- Teriyaki Dipping Sauce (see page 139)

1. Add all the ingredients except avocado oil and dipping sauce to a bowl or food processor and combine until well mixed.

2. Heat 1 tsp of oil in a medium-sized skillet. Use a spatula to spread oil evenly. With a small ladle add about 4 tbsp of batter to the skillet, and immediately swirl the skillet to spread the batter into a thin pancake.

3. Cook over medium heat until the bottom side is just set, about 2 minutes; flip with a spatula; and cook the other side until just cooked through, about 1 minute. Continue to cook the rest of the batter. If the batter becomes too thick to spread, add water, and mix well.

4. Serve pancakes with dipping sauce.

Wild Rice, Almond, and Cranberry Dressing (V)

This is one of my favorite lunches, and it is great to fuel your workout days.

Wild rice is rich in zinc, fiber, and folate. It also has 30 times the antioxidant activity of white rice. As always, you can soak and rinse the rice before cooking to reduce phytates.

Cranberries are rich in vitamin C and have been linked to a lower risk of urinary tract infections, cancer prevention, improved immune function, and lowering blood pressure.

Rice

- 2 cups wild rice
- 1 tsp grated orange zest
- 1 tsp cinnamon
- Sprinkle celery seeds (optional)
- ½ tsp salt
- ½ tsp cloves
- ½ tsp dried ginger
- 4 cups water

Cranberry Dressing

- 1 tbsp EVOO
- ½ small red onion (diced)
- 2 cups chopped onion
- 2 cloves garlic, minced
- ½ cup dried cranberries

Toppings

- Optional: ½ cup nuts, seeds or cheese of choice

Rice

1. Combine the rice ingredients in pot and heat to a boil over high heat.
2. Cook, covered, over low heat until the rice is tender (about 45 minutes).
3. Remove from heat and let stand, covered, for 10 minutes.
4. Set the rice aside in a bowl.

Dressing and final prep

5. Heat the oil in a large skillet over medium heat. Add the chopped onion and stir. Cover and cook over low heat until the onions wilt (about 5 minutes).
6. Add the garlic, cranberries and rice. Stir and cook for 1-2 minutes.
7. Remove from heat and serve with optional toppings. Serve warm.

Wild Rice Croquette and Apple Salad

Arugula is a wonderfully peppery and low-reactive leafy green, but as it is a goitrogen, please limit its use to once weekly. It is packed with antioxidants and rich in vitamin K.

Nasturtium is very easy to grow with beautiful edible flowers. Nasturtium are very rich in vitamin C and it is a natural antibiotic. It's great for colds, sore throats and coughs. It has a slightly peppery taste just like arugula.

Dill is antimicrobial, which can also aid digestion and fight depression. Dill's oil aids the secretion of bile and digestive juices and helps to fight gas. These oils also stimulate peristalsis which helps to prevent constipation. Dill is also used to help promote deep sleep.

Wild Rice patties:

- 1 cup water
- ½ cup wild rice
- ¼ tsp sea salt (plus more to taste)
- ½ cup goat cheese
- 1 egg
- ½ cup panko
- 3 tbsp EVOO, more as needed

Salad:

- 6 cups arugula
- 2 apples chopped
- 1 yellow carrot (chopped)
- 1 purple carrot (chopped)
- 1 cup nasturtium (optional)
- 3 tbsp EVOO
- 2 tbsp lemon juice or balsamic
- 2 tbsp chopped dill

1. In one cup boiling water, add ½ cup rice and salt. Reduce to a simmer, cover the pot, and cook for about 45 minutes, or until the rice is tender and the water has been absorbed. Let sit for a few minutes to absorb any remaining water.

2. Let the rice cool for 10 minutes. Add the goat cheese and egg and combine thoroughly. Form 8 patties 2 inches in diameter and dredge through the panko. Let sit for 30 minutes. Dredge through panko again if patties feel too wet.

3. Set the skillet over medium heat. Add the EVOO, adding more as needed to create a 1/8-inch-thick depth. When the oil is hot, add the rice patties.

4. Pan-fry for about 4 minutes until browned. Gently flip the patties and fry on the other side for another 3 minutes or so.

5. Add the arugula to a big bowl and top with chopped apple, carrots and optional nasturtium. Dress with the EVOO, lemon juice, and dill. Serve the salad with the patties on top.

Wild Rice Croquette and Apple Salad, page 114

Zucchini Carrot Fritters

Zucchini and carrots are Metabolism Plan staples all right—what a fun way to jazz up the same old up. I also use this base recipe all the time to make use of leftovers. Really, we all need is recipes like this to reduce waste. It decreases stress, saves time and money. Repurposing leftovers into delicious dishes makes us feel good and is good for the environment.

The eggs and cheese in this make it a perfect lunch, so serve on a simple salad, or you can make a veggie wrap with the fritters with Lavash (page 92) or Spelt Chapati (page 170).

Fritters
- 2 medium zucchinis (grated)
- 2 medium carrots (grated)
- 2 eggs (beaten)
- ¼ cup grated Manchego
- ½ cup panko (more for dredging)
- Avocado oil for frying

Sauce
- ¼ cup goat cheese
- 1 tbsp EVOO
- 1 tsp lemon juice or balsamic vinegar
- 1 chopped garlic clove
- 1 tsp honey

1. Take a towel and blot the grated zucchini dry and add to a medium bowl. Add the carrots, mix well, and then add the egg, Manchego, and panko.
2. Form into 2-inch patties. Let sit for ½ hour.
3. Add all sauce ingredients to a small food processor and mix well.
4. Using a skillet on medium heat, add avocado oil to ⅛-inch depth. Dredge the patties through the panko, place them into the skillet, and fry until browned on one side (3-4 minutes). Flip and fry until browned on the other side.
5. Drizzle sauce over patties. Enjoy immediately.

Zucchini Chips with Cheese and Panko

Here's a great recipe for some zucchini chips that the whole family will love! I can't tell you how many clients have said their kids (or spouse) would never touch zucchini. Then I break this recipe out and then all of a sudden, we have a zucchini loving household! To make these chips extra crispy you could use an egg wash, but for folks who are egg challenged, I just wanted a method that uses avocado oil as a binding agent.

You could also use the recipe for any thinly sliced vegetable. I love this with butternut squash or mushrooms.

This recipe can be made gluten-free using gluten-free panko. You could also try using almond flour. This is wonderful when paired with a soup and salad or as a side dish.

- 1 lb. zucchini (roughly 2 medium large, sliced in ¼ -inch rounds)
- 2 tbsp avocado oil (more for greasing baking sheet)
- ¼ cup finely grated goat Gouda or Manchego
- ¼ cup panko (or gluten-free panko)
- 1 tsp garlic powder
- ½ tsp onion powder
- ½ tsp oregano
- Optional ½ tsp cayenne
- Fresh black pepper

1. Preheat the oven to 450 °F.
2. Blot sliced zucchini dry with a towel.
3. Using a medium-sized bowl, toss the zucchini with the oil. Combine the cheese, panko, spices in another medium-sized bowl.
4. Dip the zucchini into the panko spice mix, both sides, pressing down to mix.
5. Bake the zucchini rounds for 15 minutes, then flip over and bake for an additional 10-15 minutes until browned and crisp. Serve piping hot.

Zucchini Pasta & Almond Butter Sate (V)

This dish will have enough protein to make it a perfect Plan lunch! Scallions boost immune function, are good for eye health, and fight cancer.

Roasted nut butters tend to be much more reactive, as roasting at a high heat can negatively affect the proteins, omegas, and fats. So, stick with a raw almond butter. It's pretty easy to make on your own nut butters if you have a Vitamix (and a lot of patience, which I don't have).

A Vitamix really is worth the money, by the way. We still have one from the 1980s and it's totally functional!

Dressing:

- ½ cup crunchy raw almond butter
- ¾ cup water
- 2 tbsp chopped peeled fresh ginger
- 1 medium garlic clove (chopped)
- 1 tbsp rice vinegar
- 2 tsp honey
- 1-2 tbsp sriracha

Noodle Salad

- 6 cups zucchini pasta
- 2 scallions (thinly sliced)
- 1 oz. crushed sun seeds or 2 tbsp hemp seeds

Dressing:

1. Mix all the dressing ingredients in a food processor and then pour into a medium sized bowl.

Noodle Salad

2. Sauté the zucchini pasta in a medium skillet with EVOO for 3-4 minutes until tender.

3. Add the cooked zucchini noodles, raw scallions, and seeds to the dressing, tossing to combine, top with seeds and serve immediately.

Sauces and Dressings

Advieh (V)

Advieh is a Persian aromatic spice mix, which is incredible for digestion. It is traditionally used in rice dishes and stews. Rose petals boost your immune system and digestive health. It is a natural diuretic and is used to treat urinary tract infections. It also has high levels of antioxidants and vitamin C.

- 4 tsp cinnamon
- 2 tsp dried rose petals
- 2 tsp cumin
- 2 tsp ground cardamom
- 1 tsp black pepper
- ½ tsp ground clove

1. Put all the spices into a Mason jar with a tight lid.
2. Shake well and make sure the spices are fully mixed.
3. Store in the spice cabinet and use for rice dishes and stews.

Apricot Habanero Hot Sauce (V)

If this is too much heat for you, substitute jalapenos for the much hotter habanero. Apricots are rich in vitamin A, fiber and potassium and are also a good source of iron. They have unique liver protecting qualities and are high in antioxidants and carotenoids.

- 3 habanero peppers (stemmed and seeded for less heat)
- 6 apricots (pitted and chopped)
- 3 tbsp rice vinegar
- 1 garlic clove
- 2 tbsp water
- 1 tbsp brown sugar
- 1½ tsp maple syrup
- ¼ tsp sea salt

1. Combine the habaneros with the chopped apricot, vinegar, and garlic in a blender, processing until smooth.
2. Simmer the brown sugar, maple syrup, and sea salt with 2 tbsp of water, and add the habanero and apricot purée. Simmer, uncovered, for 20 minutes.

Note: You may want to wear kitchen gloves when stemming the habaneros.

Avocado Mayo (V)

I am totally egg-challenged, and I gain a pound even by looking at a yolk! Here's a great mayo alternative with healthy fats, loads of potassium, and omega 9. Using raw garlic will help to boost immune function and is especially needed during cold season.

- 2 avocados
- 1 tbsp lemon juice
- ⅛ tsp pink Himalayan sea salt

- 1 garlic clove (optional)
- ¼ cup EVOO

1. Scoop out the avocado flesh and put it into the blender or food processor.
2. Add lemon juice, salt and garlic clove and blend.
3. Add in EVOO and keep pureeing until smooth. Serve immediately or refrigerate.

Basil Mint Vinaigrette (V)

So. Incredibly. Refreshing! The great thing about this recipe is that the raw garlic not only replicates the taste of mustard, but the herbs and garlic are all yeast fighters!

- 1 cup EVOO
- ¾ cup balsamic
- ½ cup fresh mint

- ½ cup basil
- 1 garlic clove (chopped)

1. Pop everything into a food processor or blender.
2. Blend all the ingredients together and serve immediately or refrigerate.

Best Stir-Fry Sauce (V)

The best stir-fry sauce, ever! The flavors are insane!!! I make this in big batches and freeze in 4-oz. Mason jars.

- 4 inches of fresh turmeric (clopped)
- 4 inches fresh ginger (grated)
- 10 garlic cloves
- ¼ cup fresh basil
- 1–3 chili peppers

- ¼ cup coconut aminos
- ¼ cup oil of choice (EVOO or sesame)
- 2 tbsp agave or honey
- 4 tsp organic orange zest

1. Add all the ingredients to a food processor or blender and mix until thoroughly combined.

Caramelized Onion Dip (V)

Here's an easy and fun app or pre-dinner nibble for your holiday dinner. Eating caramelized onions too often can kick up yeast, so save it for special occasions.

- 2 lb. onions (6 to 8 medium-sized, chopped, 5 to 6 cups)
- 4 tbsp EVOO (more as needed)
- 2 tbsp freshly ground black pepper
- 1 tbsp fresh thyme leaves
- 1 tsp dried sage
- 1 cup goat cheese
- ½ cup coconut milk
- Crudités or chips for serving

1. Add 2 tablespoons of EVOO in a large skillet over medium low heat. Add the onions and stir occasionally, every few minutes, adding more oil as needed. The onions should be caramelized in 20 minutes.

2. Sprinkle with black pepper, stir in the thyme and sage, and remove the onions from the heat. When they have cooled, add the goat cheese and coconut milk.

3. Serve warm with crudités or chips.

Carrot Ginger Turmeric Sauce (V)

Turmeric is rich in antioxidants and strongly anti-inflammatory. It is noted as being anti-cancer and in improving brain function. It is best to consume black pepper with it, which enhances the bio-availability of turmeric's healing properties.

- 2 tbsp EVOO
- 2 chopped carrots
- 2 garlic cloves (chopped)
- 2 tbsp chopped fresh turmeric
- 2 tbsp chopped fresh ginger
- 2 tbsp water
- 1 tsp fresh black pepper
- 1 tsp ground cumin
- ½ tsp sea salt
- ½ tsp chipotle
- 2 tbsp rice vinegar

1. Heat the oil in a skillet over medium heat.

2. Add the carrots, garlic, and turmeric and cook for 6 minutes until the carrots are tender.

3. Add all the remaining ingredients, except the vinegar, and simmer for another 5 minutes.

4. Allow to cool, add to food processor with rice vinegar, and blend until smooth.

Cashew Dressing (V)

You could soak the cashews overnight and then drain the water or just use raw cashew butter (see notes page 7 on soaking seeds and nuts). Cashews are a good source of B vitamins and a vegan source of calcium. Pairing this with the high protein and B-12 of nutritional yeast makes this dressing super rich in nutrients.

- ¾ cup raw cashews or raw cashew butter
- 2 tbsp nutritional yeast
- 2 tbsp rice vinegar or lemon juice
- ¼ tsp pink Himalayan salt
- 1 garlic clove
- Water as needed

1. Process all the ingredients in a food processor with a generous splash of water until smooth.

Chili-Infused Lemon Balm Honey (V)

This is truly so delicious. I love it drizzled on bread with a fresh goat ricotta or on some grilled vegetables.

Lemon balm is very effective for treating insomnia and is also known as a carminative herb, which means that it helps poor digestion. Traditional Persian medicine has used lemon balm to treat heart palpitations, and of course this is an incredible anti-anxiety herb as well. In fact, many of my clients have used lemon balm to help them wean off of anxiety medications. So, check with your doctor if you are on anxiety medications and start to use this wonder herb more often, you will both be pleasantly surprised.

- ½ cup honey
- 2 tbsp fine diced lemon balm
- 1 Vietnamese chili (finely diced with seeds)

1. Combine all the ingredients and let sit for at least a half hour.
2. Use immediately or store in the refrigerator.
3. Keeps for 5 days.

Cranberry-Pecan Chutney (V)

This chutney is a great mix of sweetness, a bit of spice, and texture. Adding that orange zest knocks this out of the park.

Apple cider is a good source of potassium and iron.

Cloves can help balance blood sugar and a half teaspoon of cloves has as much antioxidants as a half cup of blueberries! Recent lab studies have shown cloves powerful anti-cancer potential from slowing growth of cancer cells to killing them entirely. It may also be useful in treating diabetes and aiding weight loss.

- ¾ cup dried unsulfured apricots (diced)
- ½ cup water
- ½ cup apple cider
- ½ cup agave or honey
- 1 (3-inch) cinnamon stick
- 1-inch ginger (grated)
- 1 tsp whole cloves
- ⅛ tsp cayenne

- 1 12-oz. pack fresh cranberries
- ½ tsp organic orange zest
- ½ cup chopped toasted pecans

1. Bring the first 8 ingredients to a boil in a large saucepan over medium-high heat.

2. Reduce the heat to low, and simmer, stirring occasionally, for 10 minutes. Remove the cloves and cinnamon stick with a slotted spoon and discard.

3. Add the cranberries, increase the heat to medium, and bring to a boil. Boil, stirring occasionally, for 3-5 minutes or just until the cranberries begin to pop.

4. Remove from heat; discard the cinnamon stick and add in orange zest.

5. Cool completely.

6. Serve immediately or chill up to 2 days. Add in pecans just before serving.

Creamy Kale Dip

Looking for a Plan-friendly kale or spinach dip? This is when I love frozen organic veggies! They are inexpensive and a great time saver. You might not know this, but frozen vegetables can be healthier than produce you buy fresh. Frozen vegetables are picked at peak ripeness, which means they have the most nutrients. Unless you are buying your vegetables locally, they may have been picked thousands of miles away, left to ripen as they are transported. In addition, if you keep the vegetables frozen and use as needed they will maintain that high level of nutrients. Vegetables and fruits left in the refrigerator will slowly start to lose their nutrients.

Lemon zest not only helps to fight breast cancer, it also contains tangeretin, which has been proven to fight Parkinson's and Alzheimer's.

- 2 x 16-ounce package frozen spinach or kale
- 10 oz. goat cheese, room temperature
- 1½ cups finely grated goat Gouda or Manchego
- 1 tbsp finely chopped basil
- 1 tsp garlic powder
- 1 tsp onion powder
- ½ tsp freshly ground black pepper
- Optional: chips, crackers or crudité of choice

Chunky Dip:

1. Let spinach or kale come to room temp. Squeeze dry with a towel.
2. Place all the ingredients in a large mixing bowl and stir until well combined.

Creamy Dip:

1. Let spinach or kale come to room temp. Squeeze dry with a towel.
2. Throw everything in a food processor and blend (you know I usually default to the quick and easy route like this!).
3. Optional broil dip on high for 4-5 minutes until browned.
4. Serve immediately.

Curry Powder (V)

There are so many wonderful variations to a good curry. Each family can have their own interpretation, and of course, the ingredients vary from region to region. The name curry originates from Portuguese explorers in the 1400s, who were enchanted by what we now call curry. It was a derivation from a Tamil word Kari, and these base spices have been used for over 4,000 years. Thanks to these world travelers, curry spiced dishes are world renowned.

- 2 tbsp ground coriander
- 2 tbsp ground cumin
- 1½ tbsp ground turmeric
- 2 tsp ground ginger
- 1 tsp ground black pepper
- 1 tsp ground cinnamon
- ½ tsp ground cardamom
- ½ tsp cayenne pepper
- ½ tsp ground cloves
- ½ tsp nutmeg

1. Combine all ingredients in a jar and mix well. Store in a cool, dry place.

Gado-Gado Sauce (V)

I remember the first time I had gado-gado sauce at a vegetarian Indonesian rijsttafel. I was blown away by the elegance of the dishes and how mind-blowingly yummy this was. In 2018, gado-gado was promoted as one of the five national dishes of Indonesia.

- ½ cup peanut butter
- 1 clove garlic (chopped)
- 2 tbsp agave or honey
- ½ tsp red curry paste
- ¼ cup coconut milk
- 2 tbsp fresh lime juice
- 2½ tbsp coconut aminos
- 2 tbsp water
- 1 tsp fresh grated ginger
- ¼ cup peanuts (crushed)

1. With the exception of the crushed peanuts, combine all the ingredients in a food processor and blend well. Remove the mixture from the processor and top the sauce with crushed peanuts.

Herbes De Provence (V)

Herbes de Provence is a term used for the spice mix in the Provencal region of France. Thanks to Julia Child, this aromatic mix became popular in the United States. It is wonderful in breads, stews, and for infusing oils.

- 3 tbsp oregano leaves
- 3 tbsp thyme leaves
- 1 tsp basil leaves
- 1 tsp sage leaf

- 1 tbsp lavender flowers
- 1 tsp rosemary
- ½ tsp fennel seeds

1. Mix all the ingredients in a jar. Store in a cool place.

Hoisin Sauce (V)

Molasses is an INCREDIBLE source of iron and magnesium. It is also rich in calcium, selenium, and vitamin B6, which help improve memory and skin and aids liver detoxification.

- ¼ cup molasses
- ¼ cup coconut aminos
- 3 tbsp creamy peanut butter or raw almond butter

- 2 tbsp rice vinegar
- 1 tsp garlic powder
- 1 tsp sriracha
- ½ tsp onion powder

1. Combine all the ingredients in a small saucepan.
2. Place over medium heat until the molasses and peanut butter have dissolved.
3. Increase the heat to medium-high, and simmer until the mixture begins to thicken, about 1-2 min.
4. Remove the sauce from the burner to cool (the sauce will continue to thicken as it cools).
5. The sauce can be used immediately to marinade veggies, as a dip, or a sauce for a stir fry.
6. Store the extra sauce in the refrigerator for 1-2 weeks.

Japanese Carrot Ginger Dressing (V)

This is a restaurant classic and supposedly a total American restaurant creation. But even if this as authentic as fortune cookies, I still love it.

Sesame oil can help normalize blood pressure and boost heart health. Shallots contain antioxidants that help fight cancer, heart disease, and diabetes.

- 3 carrots (coarsely chopped)
- ¼ cup chopped peeled fresh ginger
- ¼ cup chopped shallots
- ¼ cup rice vinegar
- 2 tbsp coconut aminos
- 1 tbsp sesame oil
- ½ cup avocado oil or EVOO
- ¼ cup water

1. Pulse the carrots in a food processor until finely ground (almost puréed).
2. Add the ginger shallots, rice vinegar, aminos, and sesame oil until well mixed. With the motor running, add oil in a slow stream, and blend until smooth.

Sage Pesto

Walnuts are a great source of omega 3 and have good amounts of B6 and iron. They reportedly lower cholesterol and inflammation, and reduce oxidative stress and premature aging.

Some of the many health benefits of sage, which are already discussed in this book, include fighting Alzheimer's, depression, and memory loss.

Walnuts are a goitrogen, so freeze what you won't consume within a week.

- 4-5 tbsp EVOO
- 1 tsp dried sage
- ½ tsp dried basil
- 1 clove garlic (chopped)
- ⅓ cup walnuts
- ¼ cup finely grated parmesan

1. Using a small pan over very low heat, warm 3 tbsp of the EVOO, sage, basil, and garlic for 2 minutes. Add walnuts and stir for 1 minute.
2. Add the walnut mix to the food processor, pulsing until it's a fine crumble.
3. Transfer walnut mix to a bowl. Stir in parmesan and remaining EVOO and mix until well combined.
4. Serve immediately or refrigerate.

Lemon Goat Cheese Dipping Sauce (V)

A great calcium-rich dip for your potato chips or crudités. Chives contain allicin, which makes it a cancer fighter. It also contains choline, an important nutrient for deep sleep and brain function.

Lemons are a great source of vitamin C, help prevent kidneys stones, aid weight loss, and reduce cancer risk. But here's a big one for vegetarians and vegans, it aids the absorption of iron to help fight anemia.

- 4 oz. goat cheese
- 1 cup coconut milk
- 1 tbsp chives
- ½ tsp black pepper
- ½ tsp lemon juice
- 1 tsp organic lemon zest

1. Place all the ingredients, except the lemon zest, in a food processor or blender, mixing thoroughly.
2. Remove the mixture from the food processor and pour in a bowl.
3. Add lemon zest and mix.

Lemon Sunflower Pesto (V)

If you like, you could soak the seeds overnight and drain to make the nutrients more bioavailable. This recipe is great to make in large batches when basil is in season. Simply freeze whatever quantity you won't be using within a week.

- 1 cup raw sunflower seeds
- 2 cups packed fresh basil leaves
- ¾ cup EVOO
- 3 cloves garlic
- ¼ cup lemon juice or balsamic

1. Place all the ingredients in a food processor and purée until smooth. To thin the pesto, add water or lemon juice.

Low-reactive Ketchup (V)

Ok yes, I will admit it. I love ketchup, even more so than my kids! This super healthy version with wonderful digestive spices fits the bill. You could easily make this spicy by adding fresh ginger, cayenne, or chipotle in adobo.

Tomatoes are rich in beta carotene, vitamin E, and vitamin C, which greatly aids your immune system.

- 4 whole cloves
- 4 whole allspice berries
- 1 cinnamon stick
- 14 oz. low-sodium tomato sauce
- 12 oz. carrot ginger soup

- 1 large onion (chopped)
- 1 garlic clove (crushed)
- ¼ cup balsamic vinegar
- ¼ cup brown sugar

1. Add all the ingredients to a medium-sized pot; cook over low heat, stirring occasionally, for about 1 hour.

2. Strain the tomato sauce mix through a sieve.

3. Transfer the mixture to 8-oz. Mason jars, fill to 6 oz., and let cool before refrigerating.

4. Allow the flavors marinate for at least 3 hours. Ketchup is good for 2 weeks. Freeze what you won't use.

Low-reactive Tomato Sauce (V)

If you have a Trader Joe's nearby, they have a great, inexpensive, organic salt-free tomato sauce. Low sodium tomato sauce would be 350 mg or less per serving.

Oregano helps fight bacteria and viruses and rosemary can help fight bacterial infections.

As tomatoes are so high in vitamin C, this sauce should be part of your winter arsenal to fight colds!

- 1 24-oz. jar low-sodium tomato sauce
- 2 cups carrot ginger soup (page 48)
- 1 garlic clove (minced)
- 2 tbsp dried basil
- 1 tbsp dried oregano
- 1 tsp dried rosemary
- 1 tbsp agave or honey for pizza sauce (optional)

1. Combine all the ingredients in a large saucepan and simmer over low heat for 20 minutes. Let cool and pour into individual containers for freezing.

Mushroom "Bacon" (V)

Smokey, slightly salty, and sweet – what could be more perfect? This mushroom bacon is a welcome topping to so many dishes, from salads to rice casseroles, homemade pizza, and baked potatoes. Enjoy!

- 2 tbsp avocado oil
- 4 oz. shitake mushrooms (cleaned) and thinly sliced (about $1/8$-inch thick)
- 1 tbsp agave or maple syrup
- 1 tbsp coconut aminos
- 2 tbsp brown sugar
- ½ tsp garlic powder
- ½ tsp chipotle powder

1. Preheat the oven to 350 °F. Mix all the ingredients in a bowl and spread evenly on an oiled baking sheet. Bake for 45 minutes and serve warm or refrigerate.

Mango Cucumber Salsa, page 133

Mango Cucumber Salsa – Mild (V)

Mango is a super low-reactive fruit, but cucumber can be a bit taxing on digestion for some. The heat of the jalapeno and the soothing, digestive properties of mint make cucumber easier to digest. This is one of my favorite salsas of all time.

- 2 cups mango (chopped; can use frozen)
- 1 Kirby cucumber (finely chopped)
- Juice of lime
- 2 tbsp raw red onion (minced)
- 1 tbsp chopped fresh mint
- 1 roasted jalapeno (seeds omitted to be mildly spiced)

1. To roast the jalapeno, just throw them on an open flame until the skins start to blacken or broil.
2. Mix all ingredients in a jar and shake well.
3. Consume within one week or freeze.

Plan Caesar

A classic dressing from days 1–20 of The Metabolism Plan. I made this garlicky to help kill yeast, and garlic is also great for immune function. But feel free to cut down on the garlic and substitute chives if you are not a fan.

- 2 garlic cloves (chopped)
- ¼ cup EVOO
- 4 oz. goat cheese
- 2 tbsp lemon juice
- 2 tsp fresh black pepper
- 2 tbsp fresh dill or basil

1. Soak the garlic cloves in EVOO overnight.
2. Add all ingredients to a food processor and blend until smooth. Add water as needed for lighter dressing.

Protein Packed Pecan Pesto (V)

Nutritional yeast is rich in B-12, which is an essential nutrient for thyroid health. B-12 is also very limited in vegetarian and vegan food sources. So, try to include this pesto a few times per week.

- 2 cups tightly packed fresh basil
- 1 cup pecans
- 1 clove garlic (roughly chopped)
- ½ cup EVOO
- ½ cup hemp seeds

- ¼ cup balsamic
- 2 tbsp nutritional yeast
- ½ tsp fresh black pepper
- ¼ tsp sea salt

1. Place the basil, pecans, and garlic in a food processor. Pulse to combine until the mixture is coarsely ground.

2. Drizzle the EVOO in a thin stream. Add the remaining ingredients and pulse a few more times to combine.

Quick & Healthy Soy-Free Chinese Stir-Fry Sauce (V)

All I can say is, and I am sure you feel the same, thank God coconut aminos are so low-reactive, and they are so much lower in sodium than soy sauce. This allows all of us who are trying to eat healthfully to recreate our favorite cuisines. Whoever developed coconut aminos should be nominated for a Nobel Prize – I'm not kidding. This is a milder stir-fry sauce and a great base for you to adjust to make it spicier or to add more warming spices. Coriander helps to balance cholesterol, is anti-inflammatory, and aids digestion.

- 1 cup veggie broth (page 58)
- ¼ cup brown sugar
- ¼ cup coconut aminos
- ¼ cup rice vinegar
- 3 garlic cloves (minced)

- 3 tbsp ginger (finely grated)
- 2 tbsp sesame oil
- 1 tsp cumin
- 1 tsp coriander

1. Combine all the ingredients in a medium-sized sauce pan and simmer for 10 minutes.

2. Let cool and store.

Ranchero Sauce (V)

I grew up in San Diego as a teenager, then moved to San Francisco, and now go to Mexico at least once a year. I adore Mexican food and love to take traditional recipes and make them Plan friendly. Tomato sauce can be 70% reactive, but once you add carrot soup, it goes down to 10%. So, use this recipe as your springboard for many more interpretations on your favorite recipes.

- ¼ cup tomato sauce
- ¼ cup carrot ginger soup (page 48)
- ¼ cup chopped red onion
- 2 cloves garlic (chopped)

- Juice of 1 lime, about 1½–2 tbsp
- 1 tbsp EVOO
- ½ tsp cumin
- ½ tsp smoked chipotle

1. Mix all the ingredients together and simmer for 5 minutes.
2. Serve warm or at room temperature.

Sage Honey (V)

When pollen is driving people nuts, I think it's time to make some sage-infused honey. It's antibacterial, antimicrobial, anti-inflammatory, and is even good for strep! Of course, it's also fabulous for hot flashes, so make a big batch. You can have it with tea, slather on your buttered bread…you name it!

- 16-oz. Mason jar
- 14 oz. raw local honey or Manukah honey

- ¼ cup dried sage

1. Sanitize your jar and lid.
2. Put dried sage into jar and fill with honey. Stir to combine.
3. Cover the jar with a lid, and allow to sit in a cool, dark, dry place for 2 weeks.
4. Strain the sage if you prefer, or simply leave it in. Use as needed.

Spicy Coco Sauce (V)

A Plan classic!! I absolutely adore Thai food, and this sauce makes your cleanse an absolute treat.

Lemongrass aids digestion, fights infection, lowers cholesterol, and boosts oral health.

The fatty acids in coconut milk may aid weight loss, improve immune function, reduce heart disease risk, and improve skin and hair health.

- 2 tbsp EVOO
- 1 large onion (chopped)
- 3-4 cloves of garlic (chopped)
- 1-inch piece fresh ginger (peeled and chopped; about 1 tbsp).
- 1 tsp cumin
- 1 tsp cinnamon
- ½ tsp freshly ground black pepper
- ½ tsp coriander
- ½ tsp nutmeg
- ½ tsp cardamom
- ¼ tsp cloves
- 1 tsp brown sugar
- 1 can coconut milk
- 2 tbsp sriracha sauce (more for extra spice or 1-2 chopped hot chilies)
- 1 lemongrass stalk chopped into 1-inch pieces (optional)

1. Pour the oil in a large saucepan over medium heat, and after 30 seconds, add the onion and garlic; sauté for 1 minute, stirring frequently until the onion and garlic start to brown.

2. Add the eight ingredients from ginger to cloves, and sauté for 1 minute on low heat until the spices begin to smell fragrant.

3. Add brown sugar, coconut milk, sriracha, and lemongrass, if desired, stirring for 30 seconds.

4. Reduce heat and simmer for 15–20 minutes, stirring every 5 minutes. Remove lemongrass at the end with a slotted spoon.

5. Serve warm or refrigerate.

Sweet & Sour Dipping Sauce (V)

This is a classic sauce that I use for all my fried tempura veggies and, of course, the oh so famous and delicious avocado fries (page 76).

- ¼ cup agave or honey
- ¼ cup rice vinegar
- 2-3 tbsp sriracha
- 1 tbsp fresh finely grated ginger
- ½ tsp cinnamon

1. Combine all the ingredients and serve immediately or refrigerate.

Sunflower Tahini (V)

I had a dear client who loved hummus but was very reactive to sesame seeds. It's amazing how creative you can get when you want to create a recipe to make someone happy. In a flash, this recipe came to my mind, and now, it's a Plan staple. This is another base recipe that you can be creative with! I love this with curry powder, jerk seasoning, or just whatever is growing in my garden. It's great for thickening stews and is amazing over grains, helping to boost protein and metabolism.

- 1 cup sunflower seeds
- ¼ cup EVOO
- ¼ cup water
- 2 tbsp lemon juice
- Dash of sea salt
- Optional: add more water for creamier tahini

1. Add all ingredients to a food processor and blend until smooth (about 3 minutes).
2. Serve immediately or store and refrigerate up to 5 days.

Tahini Ranch Dressing (V)

There is a great dairy-free ranch dressing in *The Plan Cookbook*, but if you are OD'ing on coconut milk, you can try this variation. Sauces make the same old exciting and new again! The sauce is delish with grilled romaine and crudité.

- 1 cup sunflower tahini (page 136)
- ½ cup lemon juice
- ½ cup water
- ½ tsp garlic powder
- ½ tsp onion powder

- 1 tbsp EVOO
- Salt and freshly ground black pepper to taste
- 1 cup finely chopped dill & chives

1. Use a spatula to mix the tahini with lemon juice in a large bowl. Don't worry if the mixture starts to clump. Gradually add water and keep mixing; the tahini will soon turn creamy.

2. Add garlic powder, onion powder, and EVOO and taste. Season with salt and pepper. Mix in the herbs. The dressing is ready to use right away, although will improve with age.

Tandoori Spice (V)

The spices in this Tandoori mix are rich in minerals and polyphenols, which help to fight type 2 diabetes and inflammation. They are also rich in flavonoids, compounds with strong antioxidant and anti-inflammatory benefits that help protect against disease, aid digestion, and boost immune function. You can get a great salt-free Tandoori blend from Penzey's.[4] Another great option is Sahadi's[5] or Kalustyans[6].

- 3 tbsp ground ginger
- 3 tbsp ground coriander
- 1 tbsp ground cumin
- 1 tbsp pepper
- 1 tsp chipotle powder

- 1½ tsp ground turmeric
- 1½ tsp ground nutmeg
- 1½ tsp ground cloves
- 1½ tsp cinnamon

1. Mix all ingredients and store in an airtight container

---

[4] www.penzeys.com
[5] www.sahadis.com
[6] www.foodsofnations.com

Teriyaki Dipping Sauce (V)

Sauces are what makes the world go round. You can take the same foods you eat any day and transform not only their taste, but use as a vehicle to travel the world.

Most teriyaki sauces are just way too high in sugar and salt and contain soy. Soy interferes with thyroid function and can dysregulate hormones. Studies have shown that early exposure to high levels of soy, such as soy formula have had girls be at 25% increased risk of starting menstruation early. This can lead to many health risks.

Soy is also much higher in phytic acid, which means it acts like an anti-nutrient. How much soy is safe to consume? It's hard to say, we are all so different. But if you can greatly limit its use and not roll the dice, I would rather you do that.

P.S. this is why we love coconut aminos so much! All the joy factor of soy sauce, none of the potential harm.

- 2 tbsp coconut aminos
- 2 tbsp rice wine vinegar
- 1 tbsp finely sliced scallion greens

- ½ tsp grated fresh ginger
- 2 tsp agave or honey
- 1 tsp sesame oil

1. Add all the ingredients to a small saucepan over low heat. Simmer for 5 minutes.
2. Let cool and refrigerate or use immediately.

Tzatziki

This is for my tzatziki lovers who can't have this incredible dish because you are reactive to either yogurt or cucumbers (you can count me as one of you, in fact I may be your leader!). The fennel adds a different flavor than cucumber of course, but provides much of the same texture and provides a fun switch to a classic recipe.

- 1 fennel bulb (chopped fine)
- ½ tsp sea salt
- 3-4 garlic cloves
- 1 tsp rice vinegar
- 1 tbsp EVOO

- 8 oz goat cheese
- ½ cup coconut milk (or water)
- ¼ cup water
- 1 tsp fresh dill
- 1/2 tsp ground white pepper

1. Place a steamer in a pan with boiling water. Add fennel and cover, reduce heat to medium and let steam for 4-5 minutes until tender. Remove from heat and drain.

2. In a food processor add all the ingredients except the fennel and pulse until combined. Pour into a bowl.

3. Add fennel to the goat cheese mix and combine well. Refrigerate for. at least one hour before serving.

Watermelon Salsa (V)

Watermelon is like cucumber in that it can be tougher to digest, especially as the weather starts to cool. Luckily, you can extend the feeling of summer a bit longer when you add in some heat. I love this on rice or as a topping on my paninis. Watermelon is rich in lycopene, which can fight prostate cancer, protect your DNA and is an important nutrient for bone and skin health. Watermelon is also a natural diuretic.

- 1 cup finely chopped watermelon
- 2 tbsp finely chopped seeded jalapeño
- 2 tbsp thinly sliced fresh mint
- 1 tbsp minced shallot

- 1 tbsp lime juice
- 1 tbsp EVOO
- ¼ tsp sea salt

1. Stir together all ingredients in a medium bowl.
2. Let stand for at least 5 minutes before serving.

Watermelon Salsa, page 140

Pecan Pesto, page 134

Yeast-Fighting Vinaigrette (V)

Can vinegar have an influence on yeast? Yes. However, if you know me, I'm not about to cut out the whole category of foods because there MAY be an issue. Instead, let's try to figure out how to fix it so that we can diversify all our foods and ingredients. The simple solution for yeast is to find the herbs that fight them. This mix is one of my favorites. Oregano and thyme are also strongly antiviral, antifungal, antimicrobial, and anti-inflammatory. All that in a salad dressing? Yes, that's the genius of what is found in nature. Our very own medicine cabinet.

- 1 cup EVOO
- ¾ cup balsamic vinaigrette
- 1-2 garlic cloves (chopped fine)
- 2 tbsp fresh oregano
- 2 tbsp fresh thyme

1. Combine all the ingredients in a cruet and shake well. Store in a refrigerator for up to 5 days.

Entrees

Arepas – Corn Free

I love arepas! These delicious delights are a flatbread, typically used in Colombian and Venezuelan cuisine. Unfortunately, many people find corn to be inflammatory (the main ingredient in traditional arepas). Corn contains zein, which reacts like gluten, so if you have wheat sensitivities, note how you feel when you eat it. A cup of almond flour has 24 grams of protein, so this is pretty protein rich, but you could also try adding hemp seeds or nutritional yeast to boost it even more. It's also great with any of the sauces that contain protein in this book, especially the pestos.

Try topping the arepas with fresh guacamole and lime. It's incredible with sautéed shitakes and truffle oil (ok that is a weakness of mine).

- 1 cup blanched almond flour
- ½ cup water
- 2 eggs
- ½ cup grated Manchego
- 4 tbsp EVOO (divided)

Toppings

- Guacamole, shiitake or maitake mushrooms, or grilled vegetables (optional toppings)

1. Whisk all the ingredients together except EVOO and toppings and let sit for 5 minutes.
2. Heat a medium-sized skillet and add 1 tablespoon of EVOO.
3. Turn the heat to low and pour in ¼ of the batter.
4. Cook until browned on one side (3-4 minutes), repeating the process on the other side.
5. Repeat to make 4–6 arepas. Serve warm with optional toppings.

Arepas – Corn Free, page 144

Almond Flour Pizza (GF) (DF)

I love pizza, who doesn't? I also love a quick, easy dinner, and this fits the bill. Pairing this protein-rich pizza with a salad and some grilled vegetables is an ideal dinner staple that is sure to please everyone!

No matter what toppings you choose, or what time of the day you make it, this gluten-free recipe is sure to be a hit in your home.

- 2 cups almond flour
- ½ tsp sea salt
- ¼ tsp pepper
- 1 tsp dried basil
- ¼ tsp dried rosemary

- 2 organic eggs (beaten)
- 1 tbsp EVOO
- ½ tsp garlic powder
- toppings of choice

1. Preheat the oven to 350 °F.
2. Mix all the ingredients together and form a ball.
3. Roll out the dough on an oiled baking pan into a medium-thin layer.
4. Bake for 10–15 minutes (check after 10 minutes).
5. Remove from oven.
6. Top with low-reactive tomato sauce and cheese or vegan sauce. You can also use hemp seed pesto and veggies of choice, then broil for an additional 2-3 minutes.

Apricot Lentil Salad (V)

This would make a fabulous, refreshing dinner on a balmy summer night. One cup of lentils is an inexpensive, nutritious legume, providing 18 g of protein, 15 g of fiber, and 700 mg of potassium.

- 4 fresh apricots (chopped)
- 2 cups brown lentils (cooked)
- Salad greens of choice
- ¼ cup Basil Mint Vinaigrette (page 121)

- ½ cup Cashew Dressing (page 123) or dressing of choice
- 2 tbsp fresh basil (chopped)

1. Put the apricots, lentils, and greens in a large bowl and mix well with vinaigrette of choice.
2. Place salad greens on a serving platter. Place lentils in the center and top with cashew dressing and basil. Serve immediately.

Buckwheat Popovers (DF)

These popovers are delicious with hummus, cheese, and nut butter. Buckwheat is rich in fiber and quercetin, which helps fight seasonal allergies. Quercetin also helps fight coronary heart disease, diabetes, and rheumatoid arthritis.

Butter was quite the villain not too long ago. It's a shame, because butter is an excellent dietary source of vitamin D as well as selenium, A and E. All these vitamins have incredible health benefits as you now know from reading this cookbook. But butter has a unique nutrient, vitamin K2, which like selenium can be lacking in our modern diets. K2 is very important in enabling your body to effectively utilize the calcium you are consuming, this is of course very important for helping to prevent osteoporosis. Low intake of K2 has been linked to many diseases such as cancer. Dairy products from grass fed cows are much richer in K2 levels.

- 1 cup coconut milk
- 4 large eggs (room temperature)
- 2 tbsp avocado oil
- 1 tsp sugar
- ¼ tsp fine sea salt
- 1 cup buckwheat flour

1. Heat the oven to 450 °F. Brush the muffin tin with avocado oil.

2. Using a blender or food processor, mix the milk, eggs, avocado oil, sugar, and salt until frothy, then add flour and blend again.

3. Pour the batter into the muffin tin and bake for 20 minutes.

4. Turn the heat down to 350 °F and bake for another 20 minutes until the popovers are puffed and golden brown. Serve warm.

Arugula, Lentil & Hemp Seed Dinner Salad (V)

You can use any salad green with this dish, but I love the peppery tang of arugula mixed with lentils. Hemp seeds help to boost protein and impart a cheesy flavor. This is great with a warm vinaigrette and grilled vegetables.

- 8 cups arugula or lettuce of choice
- 4 cups cooked lentils
- 4 cups Roasted Vegetables (page 108)
- 1 cup grated beets
- 1 cup grated carrots
- 4 tbsp hemp seeds
- 1 avocado (sliced)
- Vinaigrette of choice

1. Add the arugula to a platter.
2. Put the lentils in the middle of the bed of arugula. In the center add roasted vegetables, layer the beets on the outside, then the carrots.
3. Sprinkle the hemp seeds on top. Add avocado slices.
4. Serve with salad dressing of choice.

Broccoli, Fennel and Rice Casserole

I love rice casseroles – so easy. Cooling your rice in the fridge overnight may make it a resistant starch, which can help with greater weight loss and balanced blood sugar.

- 3 tbsp avocado oil
- 1 large onion, peeled and chopped
- ½ tsp celery seed
- 1½ cups basmati rice or wild rice
- 3 cups water
- 1½ lb. broccoli (chopped)
- 1 medium fennel (chopped)
- 6 oz. Manchego cheese (grated, about 2 cups)

1. Heat the oil in a large, sturdy saucepan. Add the onion and celery seed and cook over medium heat for 6 to 8 minutes, stirring occasionally, until browned.
2. Add water to the onions and add rice. Once the rice has cooked for 35 minutes, place the broccoli and fennel on top of it (don't stir). Cover and cook over low heat for 10 minutes.
3. Place the rice in an oiled casserole dish and top with grated cheese. Broil for 4-5 minutes until cheese is browned.

Broccoli, Fennel and Rice Casserole

Curry-spiced Potato Burgers (V)

I love a good veggie burger, but it took me years to get some good recipes that didn't fall apart. This recipe was one of my first successes. Feel free to substitute curry for spices of choice. This is great with Herbes de Provence (page 127).

- 2 medium russet potatoes (chopped)
- 5 tbsp avocado oil
- 1 tsp turmeric (divided)
- 1½ cup finely diced broccoli
- ¾ cup finely diced fennel
- ¼ cup finely diced carrot
- 1 tsp peeled, grated ginger
- 1 tsp curry powder (page 126)
- ½ tsp chipotle powder
- ½ tsp sea salt
- 1 tsp lime juice
- 1 cup breadcrumbs or panko (plus more for dredging)

1. Cook the potatoes in simmering water for 20 minutes.
2. Rinse to remove starch, then pat dry.
3. Cool and then mash potatoes.
4. Pour 1 tbsp of oil in a sauté pan on medium heat and add the turmeric. Add the diced vegetables and spices and sauté for 10–15 minutes.
5. Once the vegetables cool, add them to the potato mash.
6. Add the lime juice to the potato mix.
7. Combine the panko with the potato and vegetable mixture and mix well.
8. Make 8 patties, roughly 3 inches round. Let sit for 10 minutes, then dredge patties in more panko.
9. Heat a skillet with 2 tbsp of oil, placing 4 patties on it. Sauté the patties until browned and crunchy.
10. Serve immediately or freeze.

Greek Zucchini Fritters

You could use feta for this recipe, but it is more reactive and much higher in sodium.

Thyme is another herb that I have in my garden, as it is so easy to grow and has so many health benefits. Research is showing that it is beneficial in fighting breast and colon cancer. Thyme oil is strongly antibacterial and antimicrobial. It's great for combatting food poisoning as well as for fighting colds. It also contains carvacrol, which can boost mood and balance blood sugar levels.

- 2 lb. large zucchini (coarsely grated)
- 2 eggs
- ½ tsp basil
- ½ tsp dried oregano
- ½ tsp dried thyme
- ½ tsp onion powder
- ½ tsp garlic powder

- 1 cup panko or gluten-free panko, more for dredging
- 1 cup goats ricotta or chèvre
- Freshly ground pepper
- Avocado oil for frying
- Sunflower Tahini (page 137) or sauce of choice

1. Squeeze zucchini dry with a towel.

2. Using a large bowl, beat the eggs and add the shredded zucchini, herbs, panko, ricotta, and pepper to taste. Mix well. Form into a patty. If it is wet, add more panko. Form the fritters into 2-inch patties and cover the bowl.

3. Refrigerate for 30- 60 minutes. Remove patties and check consistency. If they are wet, or you just like crispy patties, dredge again in panko.

4. Add ¼ inch of avocado oil to a large skillet.

5. When the oil is hot, add the fritters in batches to the pan. Fry until golden brown about 4 minutes. Turn and fry on other side. Remove from the skillet and place on a plate with a paper towel to drain.

6. Serve warm with Sunflower Tahini (page 137) or sauce of choice.

Eggs with Zucchini Noodles and Avocado (GF) (DF)

Adding in some fresh berries or mangoes would make this a perfect meal or brunch. Thinking that this would be a great lunch? Me too—served with a salad and goat cheese. But right now, we are thinking dinner, so I added the protein rich potato gratin to optimize protein and a salad for your raw vegetables which provide "live" enzymes.

We all know that eggs are rich in protein, but did you know that they are also rich in selenium and choline? Selenium is powerfully anti-inflammatory, which means a better immune system as well as better mood and cognitive function. Choline is important for neurological function, muscle control, and metabolism, and eggs are one of the richest dietary sources.

- 2 tbsp EVOO plus more for sheet pan
- 3 zucchinis medium spiralized
- ¼ tsp salt
- 1 tsp pepper
- 1 tsp Herbes de Provence (page 127)

- 4 eggs
- Avocado (sliced)
- Serve with Potato Leek Gratin (page 100) and a salad of choice

1. Preheat the oven to 350 °F. Lightly grease a baking sheet with EVOO.

2. Blot zucchini noodles dry with a towel.

3. Using a large bowl, mix the zucchini noodles and EVOO. Season with salt, pepper, and Herbes de Provence. Divide the mixture into 4 even portions, transfer to the baking sheet, and shape each into a circular nest.

4. Gently crack an egg into the center of each nest. Bake until the eggs are set, approximately 12-14 minutes. Season with salt and pepper; Serve with avocado, Potato Leek Gratin (page 100) and salad of choice.

Eggs with Zucchini Noodles
and Avocado, page 152

Green Pea Burgers with Ricotta and Crispy Mushrooms

I can't digest a chickpea to save my life. But I do well with peas, so this is one of my fave veg proteins! As I mentioned in the intro, some people have an issue with flax or chia later in the day. It can cause bloating and slow weight loss, so see how you do with this recipe. You can always have it as a savory brunch option.

The high fiber of peas helps to balance blood sugar and aid weight loss. One cup of peas contains 10 mg of a polyphenol called coumestrol. A recent study showed you only need 2 mg per day of this phytonutrient to prevent stomach cancer.

- 3 tbsp EVOO (plus more for sautéing)
- ½ medium yellow onion (chopped)
- 1 ½ cup panko
- 2 tbsp fresh mint (chopped)
- 2 tbsp fresh basil (chopped)
- 2 garlic cloves (chopped)
- ¼ cup grated Pecorino cheese
- 2 large eggs
- 12 oz. frozen green peas, thawed
- 1 scallions (finely chopped)
- Freshly ground black pepper
- Avocado oil for frying
- ½ cup fresh whole-milk goat ricotta or grated Manchego
- ½ cup mushroom "bacon" (page 131)
- Salad of choice

1. Add EVOO to a skillet and set over medium heat. Add the onion, sauté, stirring occasionally, for about 10 minutes, until browned. Transfer the onions to a food processor. Add the panko, mint, basil, garlic, cheese, and egg and pulse until smooth.

2. Add the peas and scallions and pulse until chunky. Form the mixture into 4 patties and chill in the refrigerator for at least 1 hour.

3. Add a ¼-inch-thick layer of avocado oil to a large skillet and set over medium heat. Gently add the patties. Fry for about 4 minutes per side, until deeply browned. Transfer the patties to a plate and let rest for about 10 minutes. Top with ricotta and some Mushroom "bacon" (see page 131).

4. Serve on salad of choice.

Indonesian Tempeh with Kale & Gado Gado Sauce (V)

I am not a big fan of soy; its effect on hormones and thyroid function can be so disastrous. However, the Indonesian style of fermenting soy reduces some of the phytic acid, and makes soy more digestible. I have found tempeh to work quite well for most when consumed a few times a month. Tempeh is a rich source of protein, and because it is fermented, is a good source of probiotics.

Papaya is rich in papain, an enzyme that aids digestion and can relieve pain and inflammation.

Marinade

- 2 cloves crushed garlic
- 1 cup water
- ¼ cup coconut aminos
- 1 tbsp fresh ginger (grated)
- 1 tsp cumin
- ½ tsp chipotle

- Two 8 oz. tempeh
- 4 tbsp EVOO
- 4 cups kale (deveined and chopped)
- 2 carrot (chopped)
- 1 yellow squash (chopped)
- 4 cups kale (deveined and chopped)
- ½ cup gado gado sauce (page 126)
- ½ papaya (chopped)

1. Add the marinade ingredients to a bowl and mix well.

2. Slice the tempeh, 1-inch thick, and score both sides of the tempeh. Marinate the tempeh in the sauce for 20 minutes.

3. Remove tempeh from bowl and blot dry. Pan fry the tempeh in a skillet with oil, browning them on both sides. Remove from heat.

4. Add the chopped carrots and yellow squash to the skillet and sauté for 4-5 minutes. Then add kale to the skillet and sauté for another 2 minutes until wilted.

5. Place the vegetables on a platter and top with tempeh. Top with the gado gado sauce, then papaya.

Italian Brown Rice Arancini (DF)

Total comfort food and oh so healthy. When you serve this with a pesto, it is a perfect protein dinner!

Brown rice, unlike white rice, still has the bran and germ which are rich in vitamin B1, calcium, magnesium, fiber, and potassium. It is higher in phytates than white rice, so soaking and rinsing will help to lower levels. Brown rice contains lignans, which are plant compounds that can help protect your heart. Lignans have also been shown to lower blood pressure and decrease inflammation. Lignans are very important for female hormones as lignans can help reduce estrogen dominance.

Tarragon has traditionally been used to help regulate female hormones. It can also fight infections such as Staph and E. coli.

- 2 cup cooked brown rice
- 1 cup plus 2 tbsp almond flour
- ½ cup ground pecan
- 2 tsp dried tarragon
- ½ tsp sea salt
- ½ tsp black pepper
- ½ tsp garlic powder
- ½ tsp chipotle
- 1 tsp dried marjoram
- 4 eggs
- Pesto of your choice

1. Preheat the oven to 425 °F.
2. Combine the rice, almond flour, ground pecan, tarragon, salt, pepper, garlic, chipotle, and marjoram in a bowl.
3. Whisk the eggs in a separate bowl.
4. Pour the eggs into the brown rice mixture, stir until well combined, then let sit for 5 minutes.
5. Shape the patties roughly 2 inches in diameter, flattening slightly on a well-oiled baking tray.
6. Bake for 15 minutes, flip, and return to the oven for another 10–15 minutes. The patties should be lightly golden and crisp on the outside.
7. Serve the brown rice patties with a pesto of your choice.

Leek and Mushroom Frittata

Enoki mushrooms are powerful immune boosters and are a rich source of antioxidants. They also lower cancer risk and may aid cervical health. Tarragon promotes overall health of the female reproductive tract. It is rich in beta carotene, so tarragon can assist in the overall health and function of the eyes and immune system.

Using a cast iron skillet means you can use less oil as it is already seasoned. Research has shown that cooking in cast iron pots can increase the iron in food – a study reported that the iron content of eggs increased by 300% and applesauce by more than 500%! That is pretty incredible especially as vegetarians and vegans often suffer from low iron. So, break out the cast iron and enjoy!

- 1 lb. leeks
- 1 tbsp EVOO
- ½ cup shitake or enoki mushrooms
- 8 large eggs
- 1 cup grated goat Gouda
- 1 cups canned coconut milk
- 2 cups spinach
- 1 tsp tarragon
- ½ tsp coarsely ground black pepper

1. Pre-heat the oven to 350 °F.

2. Cut off the stems and dark green tops from the leeks. Cut each leek in half length-wise and then into ¼-inch slices. Rinse the leeks in a colander under cold water. Repeat until all the sand has been removed.

3. Heat the oil in a cast iron skillet and add the leeks and mushrooms. Cook on a medium-low heat for 6-8 minutes.

4. In a bowl, whisk the eggs, cheese, coconut milk, spinach, tarragon, and pepper together. Remove skillet from the stove and pour the egg mixture over the leeks in the skillet and then bake in the oven for 20-25 minutes. Cut into slices and serve warm or at room temperature.

Korean Omelet *(Gaeran Mari)* (DF)

This is an incredibly elegant dish. It is also beautiful for brunch or dinner. Seaweed is rich in iodine, calcium, iron, magnesium, and potassium, all of which help boost metabolic function. Selenium also has antiviral properties and is essential for successful male and female fertility. It reduces the risk of cancer and autoimmune diseases.

Chives are used in TCM (Traditional Chinese Medicine) to treat impotence. It is also used to help heal liver, stomach and kidney energy (*Qi*).

- 6 large eggs
- ½ tsp freshly ground black pepper
- ½ cup finely chopped red onion
- ¼ cup chopped kale
- 1 carrot (finely chopped or grated)
- 1 tsp coconut aminos
- 2 tbsp sesame oil
- 1 sheet Nori
- 3 or 4 whole flower chives or chives

1. Whisk the eggs and pepper together for 1 minute, then stir in the onion, kale, carrot and aminos. Heat the oil in a large sauté pan. Pour the egg mixture into the pan, and heat slowly over low heat for 2-3 minutes. Increase the heat to medium and cook for 4 to 5 minutes longer or until you can lift the browned egg with a spatula and the top of omelet is firm and not runny. Flip the omelet and cook for 1-2 additional minutes so that both sides are browned. Remove the omelet from the pan and let cool.

2. To assemble, place the seaweed on top of the omelet. Roll the omelet into a tight roll by lifting one side with a spatula. Let the omelet cool for a few minutes. Slice it into 1-inch pieces and serve. Garnish with flower chives or chives.

Korean Omelet (Gaeran Mari), page 158

Lentil Pâté (v)

Looking for a nice appetizer, rich in protein? Here's a great easy recipe for a lentil pâté – or as we like to joke, faux gras. It is truly amazing with truffle oil.

35% of lentils composition is protein, making it comparable to the protein density in red meat, poultry and fish! Lentils are also high in iron. 1 cup has a third of your daily supply. Compounds in lentils are noted for aiding increased muscle mass.

Walnuts are a goitrogen, so limit intake to once a week. Coconut cream is the upper layer of cream found in coconut milk. It can also be purchased in a can.

- 2 tbsp EVOO
- 1 small onion (peeled and diced)
- 2 cloves garlic (peeled and minced)
- 1 cup walnuts
- 1 cup shitake mushrooms
- 2 tbsp fresh sage (chopped fine)
- 2 tbsp coconut cream

- 2 cups cooked brown lentils
- 2 tbsp lemon juice
- 1 tsp brown sugar
- ⅛ tsp cayenne pepper
- ½ tsp sea salt
- Fresh black pepper
- Truffle oil (optional)

1. Heat the EVOO over medium heat in a medium-sized skillet. Add the onions, garlic and walnuts and cook, stirring frequently, for 6 minutes. Add the mushrooms and sage and let simmer on low, stirring occasionally, for another 6 to 8 minutes, then add the coconut cream. Remove from heat.

2. In a food processor, combine mushrooms with the lentils, brown sugar and cayenne. Process until completely smooth. Taste and add salt and pepper as needed.

3. Scrape the pâté into a small serving bowl and refrigerate for a few hours, until firm. Top with truffle oil (optional but really amazing).

4. Serve with bread of choice, keeps for 4-5 days refrigerated. Freezes very well.

Millet Polenta

Millet is a grain that should also be included on your list of heart-healthy choices because of its high magnesium content. Magnesium is responsible for over 300 functions, including aiding better sleep and better digestion. It also helps to reduce anxiety, depression, migraines, and asthma. Millet as a goitrogen, should be on your once-a-week rotation list.

- 1 cup uncooked millet
- 1½ cups vegetable broth
- 1 cups water
- ½ tsp sea salt

- 4 tbsp butter
- ½ cup shiitakes (chopped)
- 1 cup grated cheese of choice

1. Pulse the millet in a food processor or blender until the mixture is coarsely ground like a meal.

2. Heat a medium pot over medium-low heat, add the millet, and dry toast it for a couple of minutes, until lightly browned.

3. Add the vegetable broth, water, and salt. Bring to a boil, then reduce to the simmer, and cook for about 18–20 minutes, whisking frequently.

4. Add butter to a small skillet and let melt. Then add chopped shiitakes and sauté for 6–8 minutes until the mushroom jus releases. Add the mushrooms and jus to the millet and mix well. Remove from heat and stir in the cheese, whisking until smooth.

Moroccan Lentils, page 163

Moroccan Lentils (V)

If you have arthritic pain or eczema, try making this dish without the tomato sauce and red pepper flakes first. Lentils are rich in protein and folate, a nutrient essential for a healthy pregnancy.

Beluga lentils are like French lentils in that they hold their shape very well.

Coriander may help to lower blood sugar and cholesterol and is also used to help promote breast milk supply. It is used for digestive issues like gas, diarrhea, and loss of appetite.

- 3 tbsp EVOO
- 1 large onion (chopped)
- 1 carrot (chopped)
- ½ cup fennel (minced)
- 3 garlic cloves (chopped)
- 2 tsp ground coriander
- 1 tsp ground cumin
- 1 tsp ground turmeric
- ¼ tsp ground cinnamon
- ½ tsp sea salt
- Dash of pepper

- 8 cups homemade vegetable broth (page 58)
- 2 cups low-reactive tomato sauce (page 131)
- 2 cups brown or beluga lentils (picked over, washed, and rinsed until water runs clean)
- 1 lemon (juiced)
- Pinch of red pepper flakes
- Greens of choice

1. Heat the EVOO in a large pot over medium-high heat. Add the onion, carrot, and fennel and sauté until tender (about 3-4 minutes). Add the garlic, coriander, cumin, turmeric, cinnamon, salt, and pepper and continue cooking for another 2-3 minutes, stirring the whole time.

2. Add the broth, tomato sauce, and lentils, stir well, and heat to a boil.

3. Simmer uncovered on low heat for about 20–25 minutes, until the lentils are tender, stirring occasionally.

4. Remove the soup from the heat, Stir in the lemon juice and red pepper flakes.

5. Enjoy warm on a bed of greens.

Nori Wraps (V)

If you are not eating fish, seaweed is a must for your diet. Being low in iodine can lead to depression, weight gain, constipation, and hormonal imbalance. If you are hyperthyroid, you may wish to avoid seaweed, as it can worsen the symptoms.

Spicy cashew sauce:

- 1 cup raw cashew butter
- 6 tbsp water
- 3 tbsp fresh lemon juice
- 2 tbsp nutritional yeast
- ¼ tsp sea salt
- ¼ avocado
- 1 tsp grated ginger
- 2 tsp sriracha sauce (or to taste)

Veggie rice:

- 3 medium carrots (chopped)
- 1 small zucchini (chopped)
- 1 cup basmati rice (cooked)
- 1 tsp rice vinegar or lemon juice

Vegetable nori rolls:

- 4 nori sheets
- 1-2 cups baby romaine
- 1 large avocado (thinly sliced)
- Special equipment – sushi mat (optional)

Spicy cashew sauce:

1. Combine all the ingredients in a blender. Place in the refrigerator for an hour to thicken.

Veggie rice:

2. Pulse the carrots and zucchini in food processor until very finely chopped (about the size of rice).

3. Use a towel to drain the excess liquid from the carrot/zucchini puree. Add 1 cup of basmati rice, and let it soak up some of the moisture from the carrots.

4. Place the veggie rice in a bowl and add vinegar, stirring to combine.

Vegetable nori rolls:

5. Place a nori sheet down on a cutting board. Spoon a thin layer of veggie rice in a thin line 2-inches thick.

6. Place the baby romaine in the middle of the basmati rice, mixing all the way down the sheet. Repeat with the avocado.

7. You can use the sushi mat or your hands to roll the nori. Brush the edge of the nori sheet furthest away from you with a finger dipped in a little water to moisten and seal the edge.

8. Use a sharp knife to cut the nori rolls or eat as a hand roll. Serve with spicy cashew sauce.

Persian Herb Omelette (DF)

Persian food is so interesting, with its strong emphasis on herbs, and herbs possess so many health benefits. Preventative medicine in Persian Traditional Medicine (PTM), is much like Traditional Chinese Medicine (TCM), taking thousands of years of information and studies and creating a holistic lifestyle which includes healing tools to balance your body and bring optimal weight health.

You can buy barberries in Middle Eastern stores. They are rich in vitamin C and aid liver health. They are also rich in berberine, which has a long history of health benefits, especially its antibacterial and antifungal properties. It helps with bladder, urinary tract, and gastrointestinal infections. It's also good for bronchial and sinus infections and is a potent yeast fighter.

Parsley is a natural diuretic, and cilantro is a detoxifier of heavy metals and relieves anxiety. These two herbs are higher inflammatory when consumed in large quantities, so note how you do with them. You can always reduce the portion.

- 2 tbsp barberries
- 2 tbsp basil
- 2 tbsp minced dill
- 1 tbsp minced cilantro
- 1 tbsp parsley
- ½ cup minced scallions

- 8 medium eggs
- 1 tsp fresh black pepper
- ½ tsp salt
- ½ tsp turmeric
- 1 tbsp EVOO

1. Rinse and soak the barberries for 25–30 minutes in warm water.

2. Wash and mince all your herbs or put them in a food processor in small batches.

3. Place all the minced herbs into a large bowl, and mix in the eggs, soaked barberries, pepper, salt and turmeric. Whisk thoroughly.

4. Heat the EVOO in a medium-sized skillet over medium-low heat.

5. Pour your egg mixture into the pan.

6. Let it cook until the omelette has set. Flip omelette and serve warm.

Pumpkin Seed Tacos (V)

You can easily substitute any seed or nut in this recipe. Pumpkin seeds are a rich source of zinc which is important for thyroid and prostrate health. They are also rich in magnesium and omega 3, which lower inflammation, improve mood and enhance cognitive function.

- 2 tbsp EVOO
- 1½ tsp ground cumin
- ½ tsp coriander
- ½ tsp cinnamon
- ½ tsp chipotle chili powder (may substitute ground cayenne pepper)
- ¼ tsp fine sea salt (or as needed)
- ¼ tsp freshly ground black pepper
- 2 cups pumpkin seeds
- 2 tbsp fresh lime juice
- 1 tbsp finely chopped fresh basil
- 4–6 spelt chapati (page 170) or lavash (page 92)

Toppings:
- Lime wedges for serving
- Grated cheese, mushroom "bacon" (page 131)

Optional toppings:
- Guacamole, salsa, ranchero sauce (page 135)

1. In a skillet on medium heat, add the EVOO and spices (cumin, coriander, cinnamon, chipotle, salt, and pepper) and stir for 1 minute until fragrant.

2. For the filling: combine the pumpkin seeds, lime juice, basil, and cooked spices in a food processor; pulse for a minute or so until the seeds are a chucky texture. Taste, and add more salt as needed.

3. Spoon the filling on each chapati, then add mushroom "bacon".

4. Serve with lime wedges and optional toppings.

Pumpkin Seed Hummus (V)

Oh boy, do I love my pumpkin seeds! They are super rich in protein and contain tryptophan, which aids a nice deep sleep. Tryptophan is an amino acid that helps your body process proteins. Your body is not able to make it on its own, so having food sources is very important. Tryptophan is also a precursor of serotonin and melatonin. Melatonin helps to regulate your wake sleep cycle and has an important effect on mood regulation. Tryptophan is used to help treat depression and bipolar disorder. It can increase the efficacy of depression medications. It may also reduce some of the side effects of drugs like lithium.

- 3 cups raw pumpkin seeds
- 2 tbsp EVOO
- 1 tsp chipotle
- 1 tsp cumin
- 1 tsp salt
- 1 tsp pepper
- 4 gloves garlic
- ½ cup EVOO
- ¾ cup lemon juice
- Sea salt and pepper to taste

1. Preheat oven to 250 °F.

2. In a bowl toss the pumpkin seeds with EVOO and spices. Place on a thin layer on the pan, add the garlic cloves to one side of the pan, and roast for 20–25 minutes until lightly browned (they will start to plump a bit). Remove the pan and let sit for 10 minutes, stirring occasionally.

3. Add all the ingredients to a food processor and process until a smooth paste forms; scrape down the sides as needed. Blend until combined, add some salt and pepper, and taste, adding more if desired.

Ranchero Pinto Beans, page 169

Ranchero Pinto Beans (V)

Instead of soaking pinto beans overnight, you can use this quick-soak method to make this classic Mexican dish. For more heat, add jalapeno. Pintos are a great source of fiber, magnesium, and potassium. They are also rich in molybdenum, which aids the development of your nervous system; and fiber keeps you full. You can use this recipe to make the deconstructed burrito with chapati or lavash.

- 16 oz dry pinto beans
- 4 cups water
- 3 cups homemade vegetable broth (page 58) or water
- 2 tbsp EVOO
- 4-5 medium cloves garlic
- 1 tsp onion powder
- 1 tsp cumin
- 1 tsp chipotle
- ½ tsp salt
- ½ fresh lime
- 1 cup Ranchero sauce (page 135)
- Optional burrito bowl- avocado, lettuce, salsa, carrots and vegetables of choice with chapati (page 170) or lavash (page 92)

1. Sort and wash the pinto beans; place in a large saucepan.

2. Cover with water and bring to a boil. Boil beans for 1 minute.

3. Cover, remove from heat, and let soak for 1 hour, then drain.

4. Bring the beans, broth, and remaining ingredients to a boil; cover, reduce heat, and simmer for 2 hours.

5. Remove from heat and let cool. Serve immediately or make your own burrito bowl

6. Optional- serve in a bowl with your burrito fillings and enjoy!

Spelt Chapati (V)

One of my favorite ways for people to start testing wheat is to start off with something easier to digest like spelt. Spelt is also an excellent source of vitamins B and E as well as calcium, magnesium, selenium, zinc, iron, and manganese. Spelt is one of the first grains being cultivated almost 8,000 years ago.

This very simple chapati recipe only has FOUR ingredients: spelt, salt, water, and EVOO. Feel free to season anyway you like, from chili to rosemary, you could really have a great, quick, and easy wrap for lunch!

You can also use this recipe to test 00 flour from Italy. Caputo's 00 was the first flour I introduced to my son after I healed him from his wheat allergy. You can order it from Amazon or get at Italian markets.

- 1½ cups spelt flour (or 00 flour; plus more for rolling)
- ⅛ tsp salt
- Herbs or spices of choice (1-2 tbsp)

- 2 tbsp EVOO
- ½ cup water (plus more as needed)
- Avocado oil for frying.

1. Mix all the ingredients (except the avocado oil) in a blender or food processor. Roll the mixture into 6 balls and roll out with a rolling pin.

2. Using a medium-sized skillet, add the avocado oil and fry the chapati until browned on all sides.

3. Remove from heat. Serve warm with your meal.

Spicy Ginger Chickpea Burgers (DF)

This dish is made with chickpeas but would also work with any of your favorite beans. Adding in greens at the end can help aid the digestion of beans. Adding in nutritional yeast means that you are getting in a complete protein (all 18 amino acids). Nutritional yeast is also rich in iron, selenium, and zinc, to boost your metabolism.

- 1 15-oz. can of low-sodium chickpeas (drained)
- 1 small zucchini (finely grated and blotted dry)
- ½ red onion (finely diced)
- 3 tbsp of rice vinegar
- ½ inch of ginger (finely grated)
- 2 tbsp of Sriracha
- 2 tbsp nutritional yeast
- 1 egg

- ¼ cup of peanut butter or raw almond butter
- 1 tsp of cumin
- 2 tsp of garlic powder
- 2 tsp black pepper
- ¼ tsp sea salt
- 1 cup panko, more for dredging
- 2 tbsp EVOO
- Sautéed greens of choice

1. Add all the ingredients (except EVOO and greens) to a food processor until well blended, then shape them into patties. The recipe should make 8 burgers. Let sit for 30 minutes. If the burgers still feel wet or you want more crispy burgers – dredge through more panko.

2. In a medium skillet, add EVOO and cook patties on medium-high heat for 4-5 minutes until browned. Gently flip and cook the other side until browned. Serve warm on a bed of sautéed greens.

Spinach Soufflé

Spinach is a great source of iron which is another important mineral for thyroid health. Cooking spinach allows you to better absorb this iron. Adding fruits or vegetables that are rich in vitamin C will make iron even more bio-available. It is also a moderate source of protein and is also rich in zinc, niacin, and chlorophyll, which aids detoxification and skin health.

- Oil for casserole dish
- 2 tsp. EVOO (for frying)
- 6 cups packed spinach
- ⅓ cup thinly sliced scallions
- 1½ cups manchego (grated)

- 8 eggs
- 2 tbsp chopped fresh dill
- 1 tsp tarragon
- 1 tsp black pepper

1. Preheat the oven to 375 °F. Oil an 8½-inch by 12-inch casserole dish.

2. Heat the oil in a large frying pan, add the spinach and scallions, and sauté until the spinach is wilted (about 2 minutes). Transfer the spinach to the casserole dish, and layer it with the grated cheese.

3. Beat the eggs together with dill and tarragon and pepper and pour the egg mixture over the spinach & scallion mixture.

4. Bake for about 35 minutes or until the mixture is completely set and is lightly browned. Let cool for about 5 minutes before serving.

Squash and Egg Bake (DF)

Yellow squash and eggs are both so budget friendly! This dish is great with a pesto; simply add a salad with cheese. It's super low in starch, so feel free to pair this with potatoes to increase protein and potassium.

You can buy ready-mixed Herbes De Provence or make your own (see page 127).

- 4 yellow squashes or zucchini
- 2 tbsp EVOO
- 1 cup red onion (chopped)
- 1 cup kale (chopped)
- 2 garlic cloves (chopped)
- 4 eggs (whisked)

- Herbes de Provence (page 127) to taste
- Sea salt to taste
- Pepper to taste
- Pesto or salsa of choice

1. Preheat the oven to 375 °F; oil your baking sheet; and rinse and dry the yellow squashes. Using a small spoon, scoop out/discard the insides of the yellow squash, leaving a shell ¼ inches thick. Brush the squash with 1 tbsp of EVOO and set on your baking sheet. Bake for about 15 minutes.

2. Place the skillet on medium heat and add 1 tbsp of EVOO. Add the onion, kale, garlic and a pinch of salt. Cook until the onion is translucent (3-5 minutes).

3. Place about 1 tbsp of your onion/kale mixture inside each yellow squash. Pour ¼ of the whisked eggs into each squash and bake until the eggs are set (about 35 minutes). Serve immediately, topping each with Herbes de Provence, sea salt, freshly ground pepper and pesto or salsa of choice.

Taco Stuffed Zucchini Boats

Chipotle is one of my favorite spices, as it has a smoky quality that paprika can impart, but it is much less reactive than paprika. Chipotle peppers are jalapeno peppers that have been allowed to ripen (making them less reactive), then picked and smoke-dried for a couple of days. Its heat can optimize your nutritional uptake from foods and speed weight loss. Some health benefits linked to chipotle are that it fights cancer, balances blood sugar, reduces blood pressure, and clears up respiratory issues. This spice is packed with vitamin A, vitamin C, potassium, and iron. You can make this vegan by subbing hemp seeds for the cheese.

- 4 medium zucchinis (cut in half lengthwise)
- 2 tbsp EVOO
- 1 tsp garlic powder
- 1 tsp cumin
- 1 tsp smoked chipotle powder
- ½ tsp oregano
- ½ small onion (minced)
- ½ cup Ranchero sauce (page 135)
- 2 cups pintos
- ½ cup grated goat cheddar
- 2 tbsp basil (for topping)
- Salsa of choice

1. Bring a large pot of salted water to a boil. Preheat the oven to 375 °F.

2. Using a small spoon hollow out the center of the zucchini halves, leaving a ¼-inch-thick shell on each half.

3. Drop the zucchini halves in the boiling water and cook for 2 minutes. Remove from water and blot dry.

4. Using a large cast iron skillet, add EVOO, garlic powder, cumin, chipotle, oregano, and onion. Stir for 30 seconds or until fragrant, then add the ranchero sauce and pintos. Simmer for 5 minutes, stirring occasionally.

5. Using a spoon, fill the hollowed zucchini boats with the pintos, dividing them evenly.

6. Top each with 1 tablespoon of grated cheese. Put skillet in the oven and then bake for 35 minutes until the cheese is melted and the zucchini is cooked through.

7. Top with basil and serve with salsa on the side.

Tandoori Chickpea Squash Fritters

The chickpeas, butternut, and panko make this higher in starch, so this dish would work well to fuel your workout days.

- 2 cups butternut squash (chopped)
- 3 tbsp tandoori spice (page 138) or curry powder (page 126)
- 1 cup low-sodium chickpeas
- 1 tsp fresh black pepper
- ¼ tsp turmeric

- 2 oz. goat cheese
- ¾ cup panko, more for dredging
- 3 tbsp chia
- EVOO to sauté
- Salad greens of choice

1. Using a medium-sized saucepan, boil the water and add the butternut squash and spice of choice. Simmer the squash for 10 minutes until tender. Remove from heat and drain.

2. Add the all the ingredients (except EVOO and greens) to a food processor and blend thoroughly.

3. Let sit for 10 minutes for fritter batter to firm.

4. Form 2-inch patties. If patties are too wet dredge through panko.

5. In a medium sauté pan at medium heat, add EVOO and fritters. Sauté on each side until golden brown for approx. 4 minutes per side. Serve with salad of choice.

Vegetable Timbale with Lentils

This is a classic and beloved side dish from *The Plan*. I updated it by adding lentils, making it a perfect main course. It's pretty much the first Plan dish that people bring to dinner parties.

- 1 large zucchini
- 1 red onion (peeled)
- 3 cups kale (deveined)
- 2 large carrots
- 8 shiitake mushrooms

- 4–6 oz. soft goat cheese
- 2 cups cooked lentils
- 2 oz. Parmesan or Manchego (grated)

1. Preheat the oven to 400 °F.

2. Use a mandolin to slice the zucchini, Slice the onion, kale, carrots and shiitakes as thinly as you can.

3. In an ungreased 9-inch baking dish, create layers as for lasagna, layering the vegetables, lentils, and cheeses in this order: zucchini, onion, kale, goat cheese, carrots, shiitakes, lentils, and Parmesan or Manchego.

4. Bake for 30 minutes or until the cheese on top is slightly golden.

Vegan Chunky Chickpea Salad (V)

We all know a traditional deli tuna or chicken salad. It's time to rethink that and make it healthy! The hijiki option is great for our folks who are hypothyroid, as it contains iodine. Just take 2 tsp of hijiki and soak overnight. This gives the salad a seafood flavor reminiscent of a tuna salad! Hijiki can help boost energy levels and is rich in calcium, iron, and magnesium.

- 2 cups cooked chickpeas, or 1 16 oz. can of low-sodium chickpeas.
- ¼ cup coconut cream
- 1 garlic clove
- 1½ tbsp balsamic vinegar
- 2 tsp celery seeds
- ½ cup hemp seeds
- 2 tbsp sliced scallions
- 1 tsp black pepper
- Optional – 1 tbsp rehydrated hijiki (soak overnight)
- Salad greens of choice or bread of choice

1. Place the chickpeas in the food processor and pulse two or three times to roughly chop.
2. Add the coconut cream, garlic, vinegar, celery seeds, hemp seeds, scallions, black pepper, and the optional hijiki to the processor and pulse two or three times more to incorporate.
3. Scoop the chickpea salad onto salad greens of choice or make a sandwich.

Wild Rice Soufflé

I am all about making soufflé for my Sunday night prep. It's perfect as a side for lunch with a hearty soup, or as a dinner with roasted vegetables and a salad. Eggs contain vitamin A, vitamin B-12, and selenium to keep your immune system healthy. Eggs also contains choline, which helps to break down homocysteine and keep your heart healthy.

- EVOO appx 2 tbsp
- 1 large onion, diced (about 1¼ cups)
- 1 cup fennel (chopped)
- 4 cups kale (deveined and chopped)
- 2 cups cooked wild rice
- 2 eggs (beaten)
- 1 cup milk or coconut milk
- 1 cup shredded Manchego
- 1 tsp black pepper
- 1 tsp dried basil
- 1 cup almond slivers

1. Preheat the oven to 375 °F

2. Using a large cast iron skillet, add the EVOO and sauté the onion, fennel, and kale for 7-8 minutes.

3. Mix the vegetables with remaining ingredients in a large bowl; pour the mixture into the skillet; and top with almond slivers.

4. Bake 20–25 minutes or until light golden and heated through.

Zucchini Latkes (DF)

Not just for the holidays! These delicious latkes could be a perfect dinner or brunch option. Avocado oil is a great source of vitamin E, a powerful antioxidant. It's also your oil of choice for cooking at higher heat.

- 2 cups peeled, grated russet potatoes (from about 1-pound potatoes; see headnote)
- 1 cup grated zucchini (unpeeled, from 1 medium zucchini)
- 1 cup onion (chopped)
- 2 large eggs (lightly beaten)
- 1 tbsp chopped fresh thyme
- 1 tsp finely chopped fresh rosemary
- 1 tsp finely chopped fresh sage
- ½ cup flour (more as needed)
- 1 tsp sea salt
- Pinch of freshly ground black pepper
- Avocado oil for frying
- Optional: Sunflower tahini (see page 137), pesto or salsa of choice

1. Combine the grated potatoes and zucchini on a clean kitchen towel. Wring out as much moisture as possible.

2. Add the vegetable mixture into a deep mixing bowl, then add the onion, eggs, thyme, rosemary, sage, flour, salt, and pepper, stirring just long enough to incorporate.

3. Form 2-inch patties in your palm, squeezing out excess moisture as you go along.

4. Using a medium skillet, add enough avocado oil to form a ¼-inch layer and set to medium heat. Fry 6 at a time, turning them over once the edges have browned. The latkes should be nicely browned. Use a slotted spatula to transfer them to a plate with towels to drain oil. Serve warm with optional topping.

Desserts

Almond Flour Pie Crust (V)

This delicious pie crust makes every dessert more nutritious by adding in protein to balance blood sugar.

- 1½ cups almond flour
- ¼ cup avocado oil
- 2 tsp agave (or honey)
- 1 tsp vanilla extract

- ½ tsp cinnamon
- ½ tsp nutmeg
- extra almond flour for rolling

1. Place all crust ingredients into the food processor and mix thoroughly. Add almond flour to your rolling surface. Combine dough into a ball and roll out. Use immediately. The dough will also keep for 2 days in the refrigerator and freezes well.

2. Before cooking, place crust into 8-inch spring-form pan and cover the bottom of the pan.

Avocado Chocolate Mousse (V)

A total guilt-free treat that's also great for your kids. This mousse is LOADED with potassium, and if you pop it in the freezer for an hour, it tastes like gelato!

- 3 large avocados (soft and ripe)
- ¼ cup cacao powder
- ¾ cup canned coconut cream

- 1 tsp vanilla extract
- 2 tbsp agave or honey

1. Combine the avocado, cacao powder, coconut milk, vanilla, and honey in blender.

2. Blend on high for 1 minute or until smooth.

3. Refrigerate for at least 30 minutes and serve.

Bettyanne's Florentines (V)

I love this dessert—simple and elegant. Perfect with a cup of tea. Almonds are especially good as a dessert option, as the protein and fat help balance blood sugar.

- 1 cup avocado oil
- ¼ cup sugar or coconut sugar
- ⅓ cup agave or honey
- ⅓ cup coconut cream
- 4 ½ cups blanched almonds

1. Preheat the oven to 375 °F.

2. Add the oil to a medium saucepan over medium-low heat. Add the sugar and agave, stirring until dissolved and smooth. Stir in the cream for a few minutes. Turn off the heat. Stir in the almonds until they are all well coated.

3. Use about a third of the mixture to fill the bottoms of the muffin wells, pressing down to a disk. Bake (on the middle rack) for 8-9 minutes until just golden brown at the edges.

4. Let cool in the muffin pan for 7–10 minutes, then use a small offset spatula to remove from pan. Transfer to a sheet of parchment paper to cool and set.

5. Repeat with the remaining almond mixture.

Blueberry Mint Popsicles (V)

Looking for a refreshing treat? You'll never miss dairy with these nutritious popsicles. Want to add protein? Try adding ¼ cup of chia seeds to the coconut milk.

- 1¼ cups fresh or thawed frozen blueberries
- 1 tbsp water (if using fresh blueberries)
- 1 tsp vanilla
- 3 tbsp maple syrup
- 2 tbsp fresh mint, thinly chopped
- 1 15-ounce can coconut milk

1. In a small saucepan, heat 1 cup of blueberries, water (if using fresh berries), vanilla, and maple syrup and simmer on low for 3 minutes. Remove from heat.

2. Let cool. Add the chopped mint and coconut milk and mix thoroughly.

3. Pour the mixture into popsicle molds and freeze for 20 minutes. After 20 minutes, insert the wooden popsicle sticks. Freeze for 4–6 hours

Bourbon Chocolate Bread Pudding (DF)

This is a super easy dessert to make. Now that I am using my bread baker, I LOVE using the old bread to make REAL bread crumbs and treats like this. Store bought bread crumbs are generally too high in sodium.

- 2 cups coconut milk
- 4 eggs
- ⅓ cup whiskey
- 8 oz. dairy-free chocolate chips (55 to 65% cocoa)

- 4 cups bread crumbs (packed)
- ½ cup sugar
- Avocado oil for baking dish

1. Preheat the oven to 350 °F.

2. Whisk together the coconut milk, eggs, and whiskey.

3. Combine the liquids with the chocolate, bread crumbs, and sugar in a large bowl. Toss to coat and set aside to soak for about 45 minutes, gently stirring once or twice while soaking.

4. Pour the mixture into an oiled 1.5-quart baking dish. Bake for about 40 minutes or until the custard has set and the top of the pudding is slightly crispy (be careful not to overcook). Serve warm or at room temperature.

Cinnamon "Cream Cheese" Frosting (V)

The cinnamon, cardamom and nutmeg aid digestion of this protein-rich frosting.

- 1 cup raw cashew butter
- 3 tbsp pure maple syrup
- 2 tsp lemon juice
- 2 tsp pure vanilla extract

- 1 tsp cinnamon
- 1 tsp cardamom
- ½ tsp nutmeg

1. Add the ingredients to a food processor and blend on high speed until smooth and creamy. Transfer the frosting to a bowl and chill in the refrigerator until it's ready to use.

Chocolate Chip Zucchini Bread

If you have someone in your house who doesn't like zucchini, you can sneak it in with this recipe. To this recipe make dairy-fee use vegan chocolate chips and avocado oil for the loaf pan.

- 2 large eggs
- ¼ cup honey
- 3 tbsp avocado oil
- ¾ cup applesauce
- 2 cups all-purpose flour
- 2 tbsp unsweetened cocoa
- 1¼ tsp baking soda

- 1 tsp ground cinnamon
- ¼ tsp salt
- 1½ cups finely shredded zucchini (about 1 medium)
- ½ cup semi-sweet chocolate chips
- Butter for coating loaf pan

1. Preheat the oven to 350 °F.

2. Place the first 3 ingredients in a large bowl, using a mixer or food processor to beat at low speed until well blended. Stir in the applesauce.

3. Combine flour with the next 4 ingredients (up to salt), stirring well with a whisk. Add the flour mixture to the egg mixture, beating just until moist. Stir in the zucchini and chocolate chips.

4. Butter a 9 x 5-inch loaf coated pan and pour in the mixture.

5. Bake at 350 °F for 1 hour or when a toothpick comes out almost clean.

6. Let cool, remove from the pan, and serve warm or store.

Earl Grey Tea and Brandy Poached Pears (V)

I AH-DORE poached fruit as a dessert. So easy. So classic. Feel fine to substitute with another liquor if you don't have brandy on hand; rum, bourbon, or whiskey would work beautifully.

- 2½ cups water
- 2 Earl Grey tea bags
- ⅓ cup agave
- 4 whole cloves

- 4 tbsp brandy
- 4 medium firm-ripe pears
- Whipped cream, sorbet or ice cream (optional)

1. Bring the water to a boil in a large saucepan over high heat, then remove from the heat, add the tea bags, and let steep for 5 minutes. Discard the tea bags. Add the agave, cloves, and 3 tbsp of the brandy; simmer.

2. Slice ½ inch off the bottom of each pear so that they will be able to stand upright.

3. Lay the pears on their sides in the tea, cover and cook for 7-10 minutes, turning the pears two or three times as they cook. Using a slotted spoon transfer the pears to a dish, standing upright.

4. Strain out the cloves. Increase the heat to medium-high and cook for about 10 minutes.

5. Remove from the heat; add the remaining tbsp of brandy. Pour the sauce over the fruit.

6. Serve warm with optional toppings.

Gluten-Free Peach Cobbler (GF)

Peaches are a total summer delight, and what a great healthy way to enjoy them. Once again, almond flour makes this tasty treat healthy enough for breakfast!

- 8 peaches (sliced)
- ¼ cup coconut milk or rice milk
- ¼ tsp ginger powder
- 1 cup almond flour
- 4 tbsp butter (room temp)
- 1 tbsp brown sugar

- 1 tsp cinnamon
- ¼ tsp nutmeg or cardamom
- 1 tsp vanilla extract
- Butter for pan
- Whipped cream, ice cream or sorbet

1. Preheat the oven to 350 °F.

2. Add the peaches, milk and ginger to a saucepan and simmer for about 10 minutes.

3. Mix the almond flour, butter, sugar, cinnamon, nutmeg and vanilla in a food processor until well combined.

4. Butter a 6x8-inch baking dish and put the peach mixture at the bottom; spoon the almond flour mixture on top.

5. Bake for 25–30 minutes until browned. Serve with whipped cream, ice cream, or sorbet!

Goat Cheese Icing

Worried that people will avoid this icing if they hear the name? Fear not, this is so good, even my son, who hates goat cheese, LOVES it. It's very similar to a cream cheese frosting in taste, but so much healthier.

- 4 oz. goat cheese
- 2 oz. butter (softened)

- 1 tsp vanilla extract
- 1½ cups confectioners' sugar

1. Combine all the ingredients in a food processor fitted with an S-blade. Blend for 1 minute

2. Place in a small bowl, cover, and let chill in the refrigerator.

3. Serve on dessert of choice.

Lemon Tart (GF)

I always think of lemon desserts as we transition into spring. Is it because spring is a great time to do a liver cleanse and lemons are excellent liver cleansers? Maybe, but that's going to be my alibi and I'm sticking to it. In Ayurvedic medicine lemons are believed to stimulate digestion and prevent the buildup of toxins.

- 2 eggs
- ⅓ cup honey
- 2 tablespoons fresh lemon juice
- 1 teaspoon grated organic lemon zest
- ½ teaspoon ground cinnamon
- ¼ tsp ground nutmeg

- ¼ tsp cardamom
- ¼ tsp ginger
- ¼ tsp sea salt
- ¼ cup butter, melted
- 18 (2 inch) almond flour tart shells
- Fruit of choice

1. Preheat oven to 375 °F degrees

2. Beat eggs in a large bowl. Stir in honey, lemon juice, lemon zest, spices and sea salt. Blend in melted butter. Fill tart shells halfway.

3. Bake in preheated oven for 15-20 minutes, or until filling is set and crust is golden brown. Top with fruit of choice.

Molten Chocolate Lava Cake

This is my favorite recipe to make with my son. When you serve it straight from the oven, it puffs up like a soufflé. If you refrigerate it, it will fall slightly, so serve immediately. If you do decide to refrigerate it, it will rise again if you microwave first.

- 1 stick (4 oz.) unsalted butter
- 6 oz. bittersweet chocolate
- 2 eggs
- 2 egg yolks

- ¼ cup sugar
- Pinch of salt
- 2 tbsp all-purpose flour

1. Preheat the oven to 450 °F. Butter and lightly flour four 6-oz. ramekins. Set the ramekins on a baking sheet.

2. In a double broiler, over simmering water, melt the butter with the chocolate. You can also microwave it. In a medium bowl, beat the eggs with the egg yolks, sugar, and salt at high speed for 2 minutes or so.

3. Whisk the chocolate until smooth. Quickly fold it into the egg mixture along with the flour. Spoon the batter into the prepared ramekins and bake for 12 minutes, or until the sides of the cakes are firm but the centers are soft.

4. Let the cakes cool in the ramekins for 1 minute. Carefully turn each one over onto a plate, let stand for 10 seconds, and then unmold. Serve immediately.

No-Churn Citrus Ice Cream

So, refreshing and so easy! Organic citrus zest is rich in antioxidants, is anti-inflammatory, fights allergies, and is rich in vitamin C. Dessert is sounding pretty healthy, right? You can make this dairy-free/vegan by subbing coconut cream for the heavy cream.

- 1 tbsp finely grated organic lemon zest
- 1 tbsp finely grated organic orange zest
- 1 tbsp finely grated organic lime zest
- ¼ cup freshly squeezed lemon juice (from about 2 lemons)
- 1 cup sugar
- ⅛ tsp fine sea salt
- 1 cup heavy cream
- 1 cup coconut milk

1. In a blender or food processor, mix together the zest, juice, sugar, and salt. Add the cream and milk to the lemon and sugar mixture. Continue to blend until the sugar dissolves (about 2 minutes).

2. Pour the mixture into an 8-inch square metal baking pan.

3. Cover and freeze until the mixture is solid around the edges and loose and mushy (about 2 hours). Stir well, cover again, and continue to freeze until completely firm (about 1 hour).

Pumpkin Spice "Cream Cheese" Cookies

These cookies are for any time of year, but of course, they really fit the bill during the fall and the holidays.

Cookies:

- 1 egg
- ⅓ cup smooth raw almond butter
- ½ cup organic pumpkin or delicata squash puree
- ⅔ cup sugar
- 2 tsp pure vanilla extract
- 2 cups + 2 tbsp blanched almond flour
- 1 tsp cinnamon
- ½ tsp cardamom
- ½ tsp powdered ginger
- ½ tsp nutmeg
- ½ tsp allspice
- ¼ tsp cloves
- ½ tsp baking soda

Frosting:

- Cinnamon cream cheese frosting: (page 184) or goat cheese frosting (page 187)

Cookies:

1. Combine all the ingredients in a food processor. Blend for 1 minute. Place in a bowl and let chill in the refrigerator while you make the frosting.

2. Make frosting.

3. Preheat your oven to 350 °F, and line a large baking sheet with parchment paper.

4. Form cookies with a spoon or by hand and press down to prevent spreading.

5. Bake in the oven for 10 minutes or until lightly browned. Remove from oven and let cool.

6. Spread each cookie with frosting and enjoy.

Summer Berry Clafoutis (DF)

Clafoutis are a welcome dessert anytime, but I especially love it when I have brunch parties. Blueberries are rich in antioxidants, they fight cancer and Alzheimer's, and are anti-inflammatory.

- Avocado oil for pan
- 1¼ cups coconut milk
- ⅓ cup granulated sugar (divided)
- 3 eggs
- 1 tbsp vanilla extract
- ⅛ tsp salt
- 1 cup flour
- 2 cups blueberries, rinsed and well drained

1. Heat the oven to 350 °F. Oil a medium-sized baking dish at least 1½ inches deep.

2. Place the milk, sugar, eggs, vanilla, salt, and flour in a food processor or blender. Mix until thoroughly combined.

3. Pour half the batter into the baking dish. Turn on a stove burner to low and heat for 2 minutes. Remove from heat.

4. Spread the berries on top, then pour on the remaining batter. Place the dish in the center of the oven and bake for about 50 minutes, until the top is browned, and a toothpick comes out clean.

5. Like most egg dishes, this will deflate as it cools, so serve warm,

Cocktails and Drinks

Blueberry Cardamom Granita

This is a great treat to cool you off on a hot summer day. If you'd like to try this as a breakfast option, just add enough chia to meet your protein needs. Feel free to sub any fruit that works for you.

- 3 tbsp agave or honey
- 2 tbsp fresh lemon or lime juice
- 3 cups blueberries
- 1 tsp cardamom

1. Add all the ingredients to a processor and blend.
2. Add one shot of your favorite alcohol to make this an adult treat.
3. Pour the mixture into four 8-oz. Mason jars and freeze.

Coconut Margarita

The orange zest gives this a Creamsicle® feel. Compared to other alcohols, tequila is rich in agavins, which reduces blood sugar spikes,

- 1½ oz. tequila
- ½ oz. Cointreau
- 2 oz. coconut cream
- ½ oz. fresh lime juice
- 1 tbsp agave
- 1 tsp organic orange zest

1. Add all the ingredients to blender and mix.
2. Pour into a glass.

Lavender Simple Syrup

Lavender is incredibly easy to grow. Being the awful gardener that I am, I planted fields of it. Come harvest time, I love to make this simple syrup and give this soothing herb to friends and family. Lavender has shown in studies to help combat PMS.

- 1 cup water
- 2 tbsp dried lavender
- ½ cup agave or honey

1. Add all the ingredients to a small saucepan and bring to a boil. Turn down the heat and simmer for 20 minutes.

2. Remove the pan from the heat and strain the flowers.

3. Let cool and transfer to glass container.

Keep refrigerated.

Lavender Watermelon Margarita

Hello summer cocktail! This lavender watermelon margarita is perfect for your parties and BBQ. Lavender is delicious and great to destress.

- 1 cup tequila
- ½ cup lime juice
- ¼ cup triple sec or Controy
- ¼ cup Lavender Simple Syrup (page 195)
- 1 medium watermelon

1. Using a small paring knife, cut one end of the watermelon in a zigzag pattern. Discard this end. Using a spoon, remove the flesh of the watermelon and place it in a blender. Process until smooth. Pour through a fine wire-mesh strainer, and discard solids.

2. Add 1 cup of watermelon juice to the ingredients and shake well (reserve remaining watermelon juice for another use), then pour it into the watermelon, and add ice. Enjoy!

3. PS: if you don't know Controy, read on (and buy some! It's great!) Founded in 1933, CONTROY Orange Liqueur, the original Mexican Orange Liqueur, is the secret ingredient necessary to create the perfect authentic Mexican Margarita.

Ginger Cardamom Margarita,
page 197

Ginger Cardamom Tea

Feeling under the weather? Make INTENSE ginger tea to rev up your immune system, the cardamom and ginger both helps to fight colds and bronchial issues.

- 4 inches grated ginger
- 24 oz. of water
- ½ teaspoon cardamom

1. Let simmer for 20 min. Strain and serve with lemon and honey.

Ginger Cardamom Margarita

Got ginger tea leftovers? Make a ginger cardamom margarita. Vitamin C and antioxidant-rich pomegranate makes this a fantastic winter flu busting cocktail.

You could also serve this warm like a hot toddy.

- ½ cup ginger cardamom tea (page 197)
- 2 oz. lime juice
- 4 oz. tequila
- Dash of agave
- 1 tsp pomegranate arils per cocktail

1. Mix all the ingredients, except the pomegranate, in a shaker with ice. Shake well.
2. Strain and serve in a cocktail glass. Garnish with pomegranate.

Hot Rum Tea

This is a great warm drink to end the work week in winter. And you could easily make this a mocktail by leaving out the alcohol.

- 8 oz. hot tea
- 1 oz. rum (warmed)
- ½ ounce lemon juice (warmed)
- ½ ounce maple syrup (warmed)
- 1 dash of cayenne pepper
- dash of cinnamon
- 1 organic lemon twist (for garnish)

1. Combine all the ingredients in a shaker.
2. Using a stirrer, mix thoroughly.
3. Serve in a glass of choice. Garnish with organic lemon peel.

Lemon Balm Margarita

Legend has it that when a mom manages to make it to Friday, there's a magical place of unicorns, peace, love, and margaritas. But for those of you who don't make it to Narnia, you can try adding lemon balm (aids a deep restful sleep and decreases anxiety) and lavender (more of the same) to your cocktail!

- 2 parts tequila
- 1-part Cointreau
- 1-part fresh lime juice

- 1 tbsp chopped lemon balm
- 1 lavender sprig and flowers

1. Mix the ingredients in a shaker and serve over ice.

Margarita Ice Pops

This is a big favorite for our summer parties.

- 2 cups diced fresh or frozen mango
- ¾ cup fresh lime juice (from about 6 limes)
- ½ cup honey
- ⅓ cup your favorite tequila
- ½ tsp chipotle powder (optional)

1. Combine the mango, lime juice, honey, tequila, ½ tsp of the chipotle, and ¼ cup of water in a blender. Blend on high until the mixture is fully combined and smooth.

2. Pour the mixture into ice pop molds and freeze for at least 8 hours or until ready to serve.

3. Remove the margarita pops from the molds one at a time and gently press the sides of the pops into the seasoned salt to lightly coat. Enjoy immediately.

Spicy Cucumber Margaritas

This is wonderful anytime, but it is especially good with the Huevos rancheros (page 32). Tequila is made up of agavins, a type of sugar that moves through the body without being used for energy and prevents them from spiking your blood sugar in response. These molecules also boost metabolism.

- 4 oz. tequila
- 2 oz. Fresh lime juice
- 2 tbsp agave
- 1 cucumber (sliced into rounds)
- ½ tsp chipotle

1. Add all ingredients to a cocktail shaker and let sit for 20 minutes.

2. Shake and serve over ice.

Passionflower Sangria

Got anxiety? Passionflower is one of my favorite herbs to use with clients for anxiety and stress (that and lemon balm). Red wine aids digestion and lowers cortisol (the stress hormone that packs on the pounds). Top that off with cranberry juice, which is a great mild diuretic, and we have ourselves a friendly little cocktail for summer!

- 1/2 medium apple (cored, skin on, chopped into small pieces)
- 1 tsp organic orange zest
- 1 bottle Garnacha or red wine of choice
- 1 cup cranberry juice
- 1/4 cup triple sec or more to taste
- 1 dropper of passionflower tincture

1. Add all ingredients into a pitcher and stir with a wooden spoon.

2. Taste and adjust flavor as needed. You might need more wine or triple sec, depending on your taste.

3. Add ice and stir once more to chill. Serve as is, or with a bit more ice.

Strawberry-Lemon Mojitos

Here's a great way to test strawberries; if you fail you may just not care. Still, you could also use this recipe to test much lower-reactive berries such as blackberries or raspberries!

- 8 organic lemon wedges
- 4 strawberries
- ¼ cup mint leaves
- Ice cubes, plus crushed ice

- 8 oz. rum
- 3 oz. fresh lemon juice
- 2 oz. agave
- mint or basil sprigs

1. In a cocktail shaker, muddle the lemon, strawberries and mint leaves.

2. Add the ice, rum, lemon juice, and agave; shake well.

3. Strain the mixture into a glass with crushed ice garnished with mint or basil sprigs.

Watermelon Cran Slushy

Mocktail for the kids; add liquor of choice for the adults. Here's another winner for any festive occasion. You can buy bottled organic lemon juice to save time and money. Do watch out for lemon juice in plastic as the acid of the lemon leeches out harmful chemicals from the plastic. This mocktail is a wonderful diuretic, thanks to this trio of watermelon, lemon and cranberry. It's also packed with vitamin C. Watermelon is a rich source of lycopene which can protect your body from the harmful effects of pesticides, helps to fight cancer and improves heart health.

- 3 cups coarsely chopped seedless watermelon
- 1 cup agave or honey
- 4 oz. fresh lemon juice

- Finely grated zest of 1 organic lemon
- 2 oz. unsweetened cranberry juice
- 4 cups ice
  Garnish: 6 watermelon wedges

1. Add all the ingredients, except the garnish, and blend. Serve immediately.

Index

Wild Rice Vegetable Stew, 71
side dishes
snap peas
   health benefits of, 107
   Sugar Snap Peas with Mint and Orange, 107
snow peas
   Chinese Snow Pea and Broccoli Stir Fry, 82
   health benefits of, 82
soups
   African Peanut Stew, 75
   Italian Chickpea Soup, 59
   Italian Vegetable and Tomato Soup, 60
   Persian Barley Soup (Ash-e Jo), 61
   Carrot Ginger Soup, 48, 49
   Carrot Zoodles with Creamy Ginger
      Dressing, 50, *49*
   Cream of Kale and Fennel Soup, 51
   Cream of Mushroom Soup, 53
   Curried Mung Bean Soup, 54
   French Onion Lentil Soup, 56
   Homemade Vegetable Broth, 58
   Italian Chickpea Soup, 59
   Italian Vegetable and Tomato Soup, 60
   Persian Barley Soup (Ash-e Jo), 61
   Potato Kale Chowder, 62
   Provencal Leek Soup, 64
   Thai Butternut Squash Stew, 65
   Thai Kale Stew, 66, *49*
   Wild Rice Vegetable Soup, 71
spelt, 42
   health benefits of, 42
   Spelt Chapatti, 170
   Warm Spelt Flakes with Mango-Blueberry,
      42
Spelt Chapatti, 170, *93*
spice mixes
   Advich, 119
   Curry Powder, 126
   Tandoori Spice, 138
Spicy Cashew Sauce, 164

Spicy Coco Sauce, 136
Spicy Cucumber Margaritas, 200
Spicy Ginger Chickpea Burgers, 171
Spicy Roasted Sunflower Seeds, 104
spinach, 172
   health benefits of, 172
   Italian Vegetable and Tomato Soup, 60
   Spinach Soufflé, 172
spreads,
   Avocado Mayo, 121
   Sage Honey, 135
squash, *see also* butternut, delicata, yellow
     squash, zucchini
   health benefits of, 102
   Squash and Egg Bake, 173
   Stuffed Figs with Goat Cheese, Nuts, Thyme,
     and Honey, 105
Squash and Egg Bake, 173
squash blossoms, *see* zucchini blossoms
Strawberry-Lemon Mojitos, 201
Stuffed Figs with Goat Cheese, Nuts, Thyme,
     and Honey, 105
Stuffed Zucchini Blossoms, 106
sugar snap peas, *see* snap peas
Sugar Snap Peas with Mint and Orange, 107
Summer Berry Clafoutis, 192
sunflower seeds
   Gluten-Free Curry Crackers, 31
   health benefits of, 104
   Lemon Sunflower Pesto, 129
   Spicy Roasted Sunflower Seeds, 104
   Sunflower Tahini, 137
Sweet & Sour Dipping Sauce, 137
swiss chard, 64
   Chard and Squash Mole, 80
   health beneifts of, 64
   Provencal Leek Soup, 64
syrup
   Lavender Simple Syrup, 195

Alphabetical List of Recipes

About the Author

LYN-GENET RECITAS is the *New York Times* and international bestselling author of *The Plan* and *The Metabolism Plan*. These groundbreaking anti-inflammatory books have been published in more than 15 countries. She has been a holistic nutritionist for more than 30 years, studying nutritional therapy, holistic medicine, herbology, homeopathy, yoga, and shiatsu. Her work has been featured on *The Dr. Oz Show*, CBS, NBC, Fox News, the *Huffington Post, Prevention, Women's Running, Fitness* and *Marie Claire*.

Lyn-Genet and her staff of doctors and nutritionists have helped hundreds of thousands of men and women reach their best health by finding their chemical responses to food, not counting calories. The Metabolism Plan is an effective way to lose weight, improve health and reverse the aging process. You may learn more about her work at lyngenet.com or follow her on social media.

twitter.com/lyngenet

instgram.com/lyngenetplan

facebook.com/thelyngenetplan